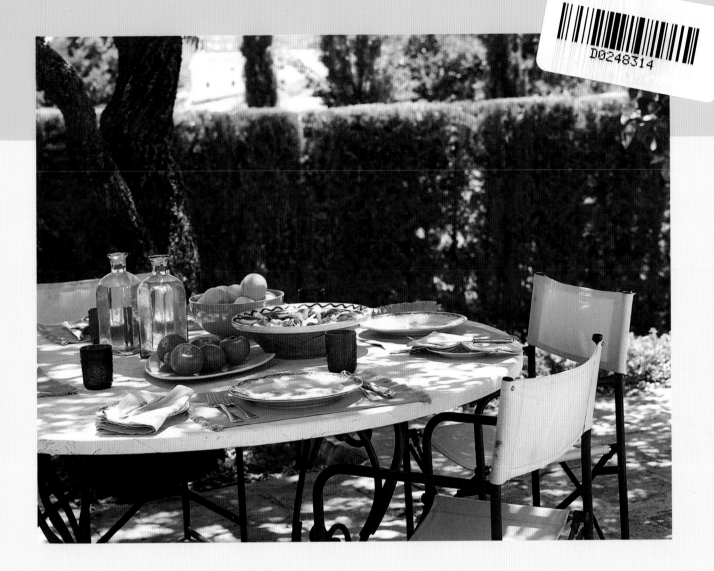

GREAT HEALTHY FOOD

GLUTEN-FREE

MICHAEL COX

CARROLL & BROWN PUBLISHERS LIMITED

First published in 2000 in the United Kingdom by:

Carroll & Brown Publishers Limited
20 Lonsdale Road
Queen's Park
London NW6 6RD
Reprinted in 2001
Managing Art Editor Adelle Morris
Editors Salima Hirani, Caroline Uzielli
Photographer David Murray

Text copyright © 2000 Michael Cox
Illustrations and compilation copyright © 2000 Carroll & Brown Limited

A CIP catalogue record for this book is available from the British Library.

ISBN 1-903258-06-5

Reproduced by Colourscan, Singapore
Printed and bound in Italy by Milanostampa
First edition

The moral right of Michael Cox to be identified as the author of this work has been asserted in accordance with the Copyright, Designs and Patents Act of 1988.

Contents

INTRODUCTION   4

1 Soups & Starters

DIPS   12
COLD SOUPS   14
HOT SOUPS   17
FISH SOUPS   19
FISH SALADS   20
APPETISERS   22
ROULADES, MOUSSES   24
& TERRINES

2 Lunches & Suppers

FISH   32
POULTRY   34
MEAT   36
CHEESE & EGGS   38
RICE   42
POLENTA   46
PULSES   48

3 Main Meals

FISH   52
POULTRY   56
BEEF   60
LAMB   64
PORK   68

4 Vegetable & Side Dishes

POTATOES   72
MUSHROOMS   76
PEPPERS   78
VEGETABLE GRATINS   80
BEANS   82
MIXED VEGETABLES   84
TOMATOES   86
SALADS   88
SAUCES   90

5 Desserts

HOT DESSERTS   94
FRUIT DESSERTS   96
CHEESECAKE   100
FRUIT TARTS   102
MERINGUES   104
ICED DESSERTS   106
SAUCES   108

6 Cakes & Breads

CHOCOLATE CAKES   112
SPONGE CAKES   114
MUFFINS   118
TEACAKES   120
BREADS   122

RECIPE LIST   124
AND NUTRITIONAL
ANALYSIS
INDEX   127

Introduction

If your body cannot tolerate gluten (found in wheat and related grains), to the great frustration of your palate, I'm pleased you picked up this book, as my aim here is to shatter the myth that a gluten-free diet means you have to give up all the fun there is to be had in food – the appreciation of flavours and the pleasure taken in sharing a good meal with family or friends. Sadly, this myth is a reality for many who suffer from this intolerance, known medically as the coeliac condition. Many of the gluten-free cookery books on the market place much emphasis on the limitations of the diet, rather than providing any useful inspiration, so it is unsurprising that people often feel doomed to a lifetime of boring and rather lonesome meals. My personal experience of gluten-free cooking has been remarkably positive – I have found that the possibilities of the diet are endless, if you alter your attitude to food slightly and are willing to broaden your repertoire of ingredients. Far from being a handicap, a gluten-free diet can be very satisfying. Meals can be stylish, sophisticated and enjoyed by anyone, not just those who happen to have an intolerance to wheat.

REDISCOVERING COOKERY

My interest in food and cooking began in my first job, when I designed cookery books with the cookery writer Katie Stewart for Paul Hamlyn, the publisher. When I was diagnosed with the coeliac condition I was devastated – naturally. The knowledge that my body could not tolerate an ingredient that was part of my everyday diet was unbelievable. But the practical implications only began to sink in slowly as I realised that foods such as bread, pasta and cakes cannot be made with any real success using the substitutes that exist for wheat products. Familiar doors began to close. But I realised that if I didn't want to settle for a second-rate diet, I would have to rethink my attitude to food.

At that time in my life I was lucky enough to travel quite extensively. Discovering how cookery was approached in other parts of the world was a great learning curve for me which opened many new doors. I became aware of the great wealth of gluten-free ingredients that I had not known of before, or that I had neglected in the past in favour of more familiar wheat-based products. I also discovered new ways of cooking rice, cornmeal and other grains containing the complex carbohydrates necessary in a gluten-free diet. I began to rely more on pulses and nuts. Things that had always been part of my diet – meat, fish, eggs, milk, cheese, fruits and vegetables – were easily and tastily combined with the ingredients that were taking the place of wheat, rye, barley and oats.

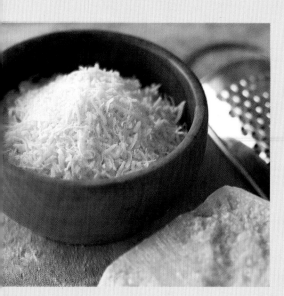

As my interest in and knowledge of nutrition grew, I became intent on eating better in a broader sense and began substituting olive oil for butter, yogurt for cream, and made good use of vegetables and pulses for fibre. My new attitude to cooking was given an irresistible challenge when my partner and I set up a small guest house in southern Spain. I was in charge of the catering and was determined (as a reaction to the days of boring and lonely gluten-free meals) not to cook separate meals for myself, so all the food was prepared without wheat. My intention was to create meals that were not only healthy, but also light, interesting and full of flavour – not too difficult with the availability of high-quality produce in Spain. Nobody seemed to notice the lack of wheat. In fact, I was well rewarded as the guest-house became very successful over our ten years there and the food, apparently, is renowned!

In this book I have gathered a personal selection of my most successful recipes from the guest-house. On the whole, these have been inspired by traditional Mediterranean cooking, in which the obvious lack of gluten first caught my attention and fired my imagination. I was keen to make my work in the kitchen as easy as possible by simplifying recipes whenever feasible, so the recipes are all quite easy to follow. Because the property is in a rural location, access to

THE COELIAC CONDITION

Coeliacs suffer from an intolerance to gluten, found in wheat, and to similar proteins found in related grains – rye, barley and oats. An adverse reaction to gluten results in the lining of the small intestine becoming damaged. This reduces the body's ability to absorb enough goodness from food to keep the body going. Besides uncomfortable abdominal symptoms, fatigue, breathlessness, anaemia and general nutritional deficiencies may arise. The only known cure is a strictly gluten-free diet.

THE GLUTEN-FREE DIET

There are two guidelines to follow. The first is to identify and eliminate the foods that obviously contain gluten. Consult your doctor as to what to avoid and use the chart here for quick reference. The second factor is to identify and avoid the foods in which gluten is an inconspicuous ingredient. Some manufacturers use chemically modified wheat flour or starch in their products. Read the ingredients labels and avoid products that contain the following: starch, edible starch, food starch, cereal binder, cereal filler, cereal protein, unspecified sweeteners and stabilisers. The Coeliac Society offers information on gluten-free foods. For more information, write to The Coeliac Society, P.O. Box 220, High Wycombe, Bucks HP11 2HY.

DON'T CONTAIN GLUTEN

Build your diet around the following items:

Fruits and vegetables – either fresh, frozen or dried. Canned fruits and vegetables may also be eaten as long as they have only added salt and water. Potatoes, rice, corn, buckwheat, tapioca, arrowroot and their products – the flours made from many of these products, along with cornmeal are all excellent substitutes for wheat flour and pasta.

Meat, game, poultry and seafood – fresh or cured. Canned fish as long as it is canned either in oil or water.

Pulses and nuts.

Dairy produce and eggs – all unprocessed dairy produce, powdered milk.

Oils and fats – all oils, butter, margarine and lard.

Condiments – salt, unprocessed pepper, herbs and spices, vinegar.

Soups – home-made soups made with gluten-free ingredients.

Cakes, sweeteners and preserves – sugar, honey, golden syrup, home-made cakes baked with gluten-free ingredients and raising agents, jams, jelly, marmalade, molasses and corn syrup.

Raising agents – yeast, cream of tartar, tartaric acid, baking soda.

DO CONTAIN GLUTEN

Grains – wheat, barley, rye, oats and their products, such as pastas, cereals, noodles, bran, semolina, durum, bulgar, couscous and breads.

MAY CONTAIN GLUTEN

These items may have gluten-containing ingredients.

Dairy produce – all cheese-based spreads, yogurt, processed milk products.

Condiments and flavourings – pepper compounds, mustard powder, soy sauce, all prepared sauces, pickles, chutneys, salad dressings and stock cubes.

Meat, game, poultry and seafood – all canned, precooked and packaged products, such as pâté, sausages and sausage rolls, and coated, frozen fish.

Cakes, confectionery, desserts and preserves – all precooked and packaged cakes, pastries and biscuits, all sweets and chocolates, mincemeat, peanut butter, lemon curd, all ready-made desserts.

Miscellaneous – baking powder.

NUTRITIONAL KNOW HOW

A sufficient intake of protein is vital to good health and especially important in the diets of children and pregnant or breastfeeding women. In an ordinary diet, protein will come from dairy produce, eggs, meat, fish, and bread and flour. The coeliac has to watch his or her protein levels, as intake will be reduced due to gluten-intolerance – the vegetarian or vegan coeliac must be even more vigilant. Make sure you consume extra dairy products, eggs, meat and fish. Pulses combined with nuts also yield protein.

Wheat products also contain energy-producing carbohydrates that must be replaced in the diet of a coeliac. Substitute these with gluten-free flour, rice, potatoes, sugars and fats.

specialised gluten-free products was impossible, so hardly any are required for the recipes included in this book (see the notes on ingredients, opposite). Each chapter contains a mixture of recipes that make excellent family fare, as well as those that are suited to entertaining. Chapter 1, for instance, provides a good range of soups and starters for all seasons, both rustic and sophisticated. In Chapter 2, you will find a collection of light meals, all of which are ideal for either lunch or a light evening meal. This chapter also contains useful advice on how to make the most of rice and polenta – both staple alternatives to wheat – and also contains a section on pulses. In Chapter 3, a range of healthy and satisfying main meals will tempt your palate. Chapter 4 contains a selection of dishes that can be served either as vegetarian main meals, or as vegetable side dishes, depending on the quantities you make, of course. This section will be useful to refer to time and time again when looking for the perfect accompaniment to a meal. I have also included in this chapter a small section on gluten-free savoury sauces. Chapter 5 contains all my favourite desserts! There are gluten-free fruit tarts, meringues, iced desserts and so on. The flavours of the Mediterranean come through strongly here, in recipes that marry figs with honey and wine, or oranges with dates. I wish someone had given me a copy of Chapter 6 – Cakes & Breads – when I was first diagnosed with the coeliac condition – it wouldn't have seemed nearly as bad then! This is my wheat-free approach to baking that many of our guests enjoyed – I hope you do too! Throughout the book I have suggested ways in which recipes can be varied to produce different, yet equally delicious results.

Although the main inspiration for these recipes is both the wealth and the quality of the ingredients and traditional cooking of the Mediterranean, I must also acknowledge the invaluable guidance of some of the most renowned cooks of our time in the compilation of this book, most notably of Elizabeth David, Claudia Roden and Delia Smith.

NOTES ON INGREDIENTS

The majority of the ingredients used in this book are readily available in grocery stores, supermarkets or failing that, health food stores. When purchasing baking powder, stock cubes and mustard, it is important to remember that they may not be gluten-free as manufacturers often add flours and wheat products to aid the preparation process. (French mustard is usually gluten-free, so I have used Dijon mustard in my recipes.) When buying these products, always read the labels to identity suspect ingredients (see page 7).

1

Soups & Starters

DIPS

COLD SOUPS

HOT SOUPS

FISH SOUPS

FISH SALADS

APPETISERS

ROULADES, MOUSSES & TERRINES

TZATZIKI

1 large cucumber, peeled

Salt to taste

250 ml Greek yogurt

2 cloves garlic, peeled and crushed

Chopped fresh mint (optional)

Olive oil for drizzling

This delicious cucumber, yogurt and garlic dip is a popular Greek starter that can be served with crudités and crisps or used as a relish for many main dishes such as kebabs, grilled fish or vegetables.

Grate the peeled cucumber and sprinkle with salt – this draws out excess moisture. Leave the cucumber to drain in a sieve for at least 1 hour. Transfer the cucumber to a bowl and mix in the yogurt, crushed garlic and chopped fresh mint (if using). Drizzle olive oil over the dip and chill before serving.

HUMMUS

225 g chickpeas (cooked or canned)

5 tablespoons Tahini

2–3 cloves garlic, crushed

Juice of 1 lemon

4 tablespoons olive oil, plus extra for drizzling

Salt and pepper to taste

Paprika and chopped fresh parsley to garnish

Tahini added to a base of chickpea purée gives this popular Middle Eastern dip its distinctively strong flavour (see right, in bowl).

1 If using dried chickpeas, soak them overnight, then boil them in plenty of water until tender.

2 Drain the cooked or canned chickpeas and set aside the liquid. Place the chickpeas in a bowl with the other ingredients. Mash with a fork into a thick purée or blend in a food processor. If the paste seems too thick, use some of the chickpea cooking water (or liquid from the can) to dilute it. The consistency should be like that of mashed potatoes. Season to taste.

3 Spoon the hummus into a bowl, drizzle a little olive oil over it and sprinkle with a pinch of paprika and some parsley. Place the bowl in the centre of a large dish and surround with crudités, crisps and tortilla chips to serve.

GUACAMOLE

2 ripe avocados

Juice of 1 lemon or 2 limes

1 small tomato, finely chopped

1 small green pepper, deseeded and finely chopped

1 shallot, peeled and finely chopped

Handful of chopped fresh coriander

Dash of Tabasco sauce (or pinch of chilli powder)

Good as a dip, sauce, topping or side dish, this Mexican speciality is made of mashed avocados, lemon or lime juice and various seasonings (see right, on plate). I like it quite spicy but you can tailor it to suit your own taste. Serve guacamole with crudités, poppadums or tortilla chips. It is especially delicious with fresh prawns – peel them, but leave the tails on so they are easier to hold and dip.

Mash the avocados roughly with a fork and add the lemon or lime juice. Mix in the rest of the ingredients to create a smooth but textured consistency. Season the guacamole to taste with the Tabasco sauce (or chilli powder) – bear in mind that this dip should be fairly hot but not fiery. To store before serving, cover tightly and closely and refrigerate to prevent the avocado flesh from discolouring.

SERVING DIPS

Dips are great for informal first courses and as tasty additions to a light lunch or picnic. There are many gluten-free alternatives to the breads that usually accompany these dips. Crudités (chopped raw vegetables) are the perfect accompaniment as well as being very nourishing. Poppadums (which are made from gram or lentil flour and are therefore gluten-free) make a tasty alternative to crisps and tortilla chips. To add a touch of class, prawns – with the tails left on – are great for dipping.

There are no firm rules for following these recipes. What I have set out to do is give basic guidelines for some well known appetisers. Herbs, oil, garlic, pepper, lemon juice or other ingredients can be replaced, added or taken away, according to individual taste. The recipes given here should each make enough for approximately 4 servings.

TAPENADE

This Provençal paste, made from black olives, capers and anchovies, can be served with a variety of crudités or used as an accompaniment to meat and fish dishes.

1   Drain the pitted black olives and blend in a food processor very briefly until they are roughly chopped. Alternatively, chop them by hand into very small pieces.

2   Add the capers, chopped anchovies (with oil from the tin), garlic, olive oil, lemon juice and herbs. Process or mash into a fairly rough paste – this dip should not be too smooth. Season generously with freshly ground black pepper. (Salt may not be necessary as the anchovies are very salty.) Serve with tortilla chips or a variety of crudités.

350 g black olives, pitted

3 tablespoons capers

50 g can anchovy fillets, chopped

1 clove garlic, crushed

4 tablespoons extra virgin olive oil

Juice of 1 lemon

10–12 leaves basil, finely shredded, or dried oregano

Black pepper to taste

MELON & YOGURT SOUP

1 melon, medium-sized (any variety)

125 ml (small carton) plain yogurt

3 tablespoons lemon juice

1 teaspoon grated fresh ginger

Chopped fresh mint to serve

Serves 4

This low-calorie soup has a refreshing clean taste. The fact that it is quick to make also recommends it, especially for last-minute meals.

1 Cut the melon in half, remove the seeds and scoop out the flesh. You should have approximately 1 litre of melon pulp.

2 Mix together the melon, yogurt, lemon juice and ginger in a food processor or with a hand whisk and chill well until ready to serve. Sprinkle with chopped fresh mint before serving.

GAZPACHO

1 kg ripe tomatoes, peeled and chopped

1 small cucumber, peeled and chopped

1 small green pepper, chopped

2 cloves garlic, peeled and crushed

Pinch of salt

4 tablespoons sherry (or wine) vinegar

125 ml light olive oil

Chopped cucumber, onion, pepper, tomatoes and hard-boiled eggs to serve

Serves 4–5 (makes 1 litre)

The best of all summertime soups! The traditional Andalusian recipe uses stale breadcrumbs, but this gluten-free version works equally well without them.

1 Place the chopped vegetables along with the crushed garlic, salt and vinegar in a food processor and blend thoroughly. If working without a food processor, grind down the vegetables in a mortar with a pestle.

2 Gradually add the olive oil and continue blending or stirring the mixture until it is smooth and creamy. If the consistency is too thick, dilute it with a little water.

3 Chill well before serving. When ready to serve, add chopped cucumber, onion, red or green pepper, hard-boiled eggs, tomato and a few Polenta Croutons (see page 47).

AJO BLANCO

200 g peeled and blanched almonds

4 cloves garlic, peeled

500 ml water or milk

Pinch of salt

150 ml light olive oil

2 tablespoons sherry vinegar

Grapes, melon balls or diced apple to serve

Serves 4

A creamy white garlic soup (see right), this is usually made with stale bread. As with gazpacho, I do not add the bread, nevertheless the result is simply delicious.

1 Blend the almonds, garlic, water (or milk, which makes a richer soup) and salt in a food processor. Alternatively, crush the almonds and garlic in a mortar with a pestle and mix with the water or milk and salt.

2 Gradually stir in the oil, then the vinegar. Add more salt if necessary. This soup is traditionally served with sliced grapes, but melon balls or diced apples are equally good.

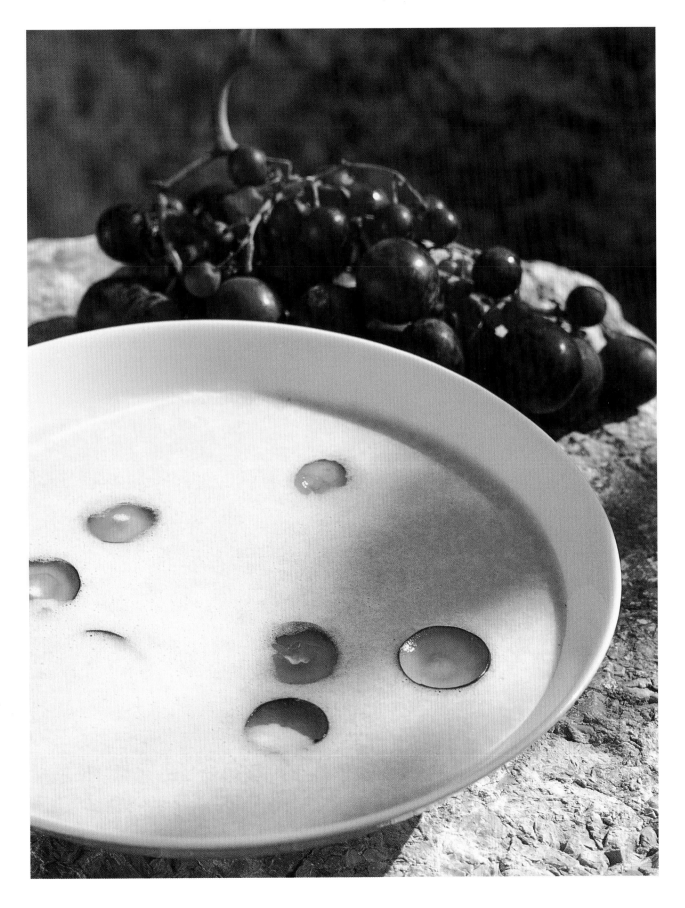

CARROT & ORANGE SOUP

1 onion, medium-sized, peeled

500 g carrots

2 tablespoons olive oil

800 ml chicken or vegetable stock

1 teaspoon sugar

Salt and white pepper to taste

Juice of 4 oranges

Chopped fresh mint or snipped chives
to garnish

Serves 6

The oranges give this soup a very clean and crisp taste. Carrot and orange soup is perfectly refreshing for a hot summer's day and delicious served sprinkled with chopped fresh mint or chives.

1 Chop the onion and carrots and place in a saucepan. Add the oil and sweat the vegetables for roughly 10 minutes. (To sweat the food, cover the pan with the saucepan lid to allow the food to cook in its own juices without browning.)

2 Pour in the stock. Add the sugar, salt and pepper. Bring to a boil and simmer covered for 1 hour or until the carrots are very soft.

3 Remove from the heat and purée the mixture in a food processor or pass through a sieve, then allow to cool.

4 Add the orange juice, then chill thoroughly in the refrigerator. Serve garnished with mint or chives.

AUBERGINE SOUP

1 kg aubergines (3 or 4, depending
on size)

1 large onion, peeled

1 red pepper, deseeded

2 ripe tomatoes, medium-sized

4 tablespoons olive oil

Salt and black pepper to taste

2 cloves garlic, peeled and chopped

1 teaspoon dried thyme

1 teaspoon dried oregano

1 bay leaf

1 litre vegetable or chicken stock

Juice of 1 lemon

Saffron Mayonnaise (see page 19) or
sour cream to serve

Serves 4

The roasted vegetables and garlic give this soup its unique flavour which can be enjoyed either hot or cold.

1 Preheat the oven to 200°C, gas mark 6. Chop all the vegetables roughly and brush them with some of the olive oil. Add salt and freshly ground pepper and place them in a fairly deep roasting tin. Put in the top of the oven, where it is hottest, for 30 minutes or until the edges of the vegetables are slightly charred, which will give the soup a strong flavour.

2 In a large saucepan, gently fry the chopped garlic with the herbs in the remaining oil for about 5 minutes until browned.

3 Add the roasted vegetables to the garlic and herbs and stir well until thoroughly mixed.

4 Add the stock and slowly bring to a boil. Simmer covered for about 30–40 minutes until the vegetables are thoroughly cooked and soft.

5 Remove from the heat and place in a food processor or pass through a sieve to purée. Add the lemon juice and adjust the seasoning to taste.

6 If serving the soup cold, chill in the refrigerator, then present with a dollop of Saffron Mayonnaise (see page 19) on each portion. A swirl of sour cream goes well with a hot serving.

SPINACH & LEMON SOUP

The flavours of the lemon and garlic complement the spinach in this lively starter. A swirl of sour cream adds an extra tang to the appeal.

1 If using fresh spinach, wash the leaves and remove any large stalks. Melt the butter in a large saucepan and add the onion and garlic. Sweat covered until translucent, not browned. Add the spinach and continue to cook for a further 5 minutes.

2 Pour the chicken stock over the vegetables, season with salt and pepper, then cook for a further 10 minutes until the vegetables are soft.

3 Remove from the heat and place in a food processor or pass through a sieve to purée. Adjust the seasoning and add the lemon juice. Reheat and serve with a spiral of sour cream and a sprinkling of grated nutmeg.

500 g fresh (or 250 g frozen) spinach

50 g butter

1 onion, peeled and chopped

2 cloves garlic, peeled and crushed

800 ml chicken stock

Salt and pepper to taste

Juice of 1 lemon

Sour cream and grated nutmeg to serve

Serves 4

RICH TOMATO SOUP

This combination of cooked tomatoes and crème fraîche or pesto creates a rich, filling soup (see right) which can be both a winter warmer or a refreshing summer starter, as it can be served either hot or cold.

1 Chop the vegetables roughly. If the tomatoes are not fully ripe, enhance the flavour by adding a few sun-dried tomatoes that have been soaked in hot water for 1–2 hours.

2 Place all the vegetables in a large saucepan and add the garlic, olive oil and bay leaves, followed by the peppercorns and salt. Cover and stew gently in the pan for 1 hour or until all the vegetables are very soft and pulpy. Stir the mixture occasionally during cooking to ensure it does not stick to the bottom of the pan, but do not add water or stock as the tomatoes contain enough liquid to make the soup.

3 Once all the vegetables are soft and thoroughly cooked, take off the heat, remove and discard the bay leaves and place the cooked vegetables in a food processor or pass through a sieve to purée.

4 Adjust the salt to taste, if necessary. If serving hot, add a swirl of crème fraîche to each serving; if serving cold, a tablespoon of Pesto Sauce (see page 90) can be added for extra flavour and colour. A mixture of both crème fraîche and pesto swirled on the top also makes a delicious and attractive garnish.

1 kg very ripe tomatoes

1 large carrot, washed

1 onion, medium-sized, peeled

3 sticks celery, with leaves left on

1 clove garlic, peeled and chopped

1 tablespoon olive oil

2 bay leaves

A few peppercorns

Salt to taste

Serves 4

SWEETCORN SOUP WITH CHILLI SAUCE

FOR THE SOUP

4 fresh corn cobs (400 g canned or frozen)

50 g butter or 2 tablespoons olive oil

1 onion, medium-sized, peeled and chopped

1 litre vegetable or chicken stock

Salt and pepper to taste

FOR THE CHILLI SAUCE

6 red chillies, deseeded and chopped

1 clove garlic, peeled and crushed

Handful of chopped fresh parsley

Pinch of salt

120 ml extra virgin olive oil

Serves 4

This sweet soup works brilliantly with a hot flash of chilli sauce (see above), which enlivens the taste with a Latin American flavour.

1 To cook the corn cobs, place them in a large saucepan of water and boil for 15 minutes. (If using frozen corn, cook according to packet instructions.) Once cooked, strip the corn kernels from the cob with a sharp knife.

2 Place the butter or olive oil in a saucepan and gently sweat the chopped onion for a few minutes until translucent. Add the corn, stir well and cook for a few more minutes.

3 Add the stock and gradually bring to a boil. Simmer covered for about 20–30 minutes or until the corn is tender.

4 Once cooked, season with salt and pepper, then blend in a food processor. For a smoother soup pass through a sieve or a mouli. Adjust the seasoning to taste. Allow to cool and chill, if serving cold.

5 To make the chilli sauce, pound the chillies, garlic, parsley and salt roughly in a mortar with a pestle, working in the oil a little at a time.

6 If serving hot, return the soup to the saucepan and slowly reheat. Serve the soup either hot or cold with a swirl of chilli sauce.

AVGOLEMONO SOUP

This popular Greek soup has a light, lemony flavour, yet the addition of the rice and eggs makes it a satisfying starter.

1   Boil the rice in the stock for 12–15 minutes until tender. Once cooked, leave the rice in the liquid. Beat the egg yolks with the lemon juice in a bowl. Add a little of the hot stock and beat again.

2   Pour the egg mixture into the hot rice broth and whisk vigorously until thickened, ensuring the mixture does not boil (or the eggs will curdle). Once heated through, serve immediately, garnished with the parsley.

50 g long-grain rice

1 litre chicken stock

4 egg yolks

Juice of 1 lemon

Chopped fresh parsley to garnish

Serves 4

FISH SOUP WITH ARTICHOKES

The success of this soup depends entirely on the quality of the fish stock. For best results I always recommend a home-made stock prepared from fresh bones and trimmings.

1   Prepare the fish stock (see below) in advance. To make the soup, place the monkfish pieces and the quartered artichoke hearts in boiling fish stock. Add the saffron, reduce the heat and simmer for 20 minutes until the artichokes are tender and the fish is cooked.

2   Serve immediately with a dollop of Saffron Mayonnaise (see below) and sprinkled with chopped fresh parsley.

1 litre fish stock

200 g monkfish, deboned and cut into pieces

200 g artichoke hearts, quartered (fresh or canned)

Pinch of saffron

Saffron Mayonnaise (see below) and chopped fresh parsley to serve

Serves 4–5

SAFFRON MAYONNAISE
Follow the recipe for Garlic Mayonnaise (see page 90), adding a pinch of dried and powdered saffron (see below). Saffron mayonnaise tastes wonderful in many soups and with shellfish.

DRIED AND POWDERED SAFFRON
To maximize the flavour and colour of saffron, dry strands by wrapping them in foil and placing them in a moderate oven for 10 minutes. Once cool, powder them with your fingers. Use to flavour sauces and rice.

FISH STOCK
Break up 500 g of fish bones and trimmings, wash thoroughly and place in a large saucepan with 1 litre of cold water and 125 ml of dry white wine. Add a teaspoon of salt and bring to a boil. Peel and chop 1 small onion, 2 cloves of garlic, 2 sticks of celery and 1 carrot. Once the liquid boils, add the vegetables with a handful of chopped fresh parsley, 1 bay leaf and 6 white peppercorns. Simmer covered for 20 minutes, until all the vegetables are soft. Strain and use as a base for soups, sauces and casseroles. Fish stock keeps well in a container for up to 2 days in the refrigerator or can be frozen for up to 3 months.

SQUID SALAD

The flavour of the squid is delicately set off by the chilli, lemon and garlic dressing in this starter that is good for any special occasion.

500 g baby squid

Juice of 1 lemon

300 ml olive oil

6 cloves garlic, peeled and sliced

3 green chillies, deseeded and sliced

Salt and black pepper to taste

1 lemon cut into wedges to serve

Serves 4

1   Clean the squid thoroughly in cold water and slice the bodies into 1 cm-thick rings.

2   Pour the lemon juice into a pan of boiling water and plunge the squid into the water for 1 minute only, then drain immediately. Do not overcook the squid or it will become tough.

3   Heat the oil in a separate saucepan until very hot. Drop in the sliced garlic and chillies and fry them for 1 minute or so until the garlic turns golden brown and the chillies are crispy. Remove from the heat and allow to cool.

4   Season the cooked squid with salt and plenty of freshly ground black pepper. Pour the cooled oil, garlic and chilli mixture over the squid and mix well to ensure that all of the squid is covered in the dressing. Divide the squid into 4 portions and serve with lemon wedges and a watercress and rocket salad.

SEAFOOD SALAD

Fresh mussels, squid and prawns dressed in garlic and lemon make a substantial starter or a delicious light lunch. I love to use a mixture of crisp lettuce leaves to complement the fish in this salad.

1 kg mussels

250 g baby squid

250 g prawns

2 sticks celery, chopped

2 cloves garlic, crushed

2 tablespoons olive oil

Juice of 1 lemon

Salt and pepper to taste

1 lettuce of any variety, chopped

Chopped fresh parsley to garnish

Serves 4

1   Thoroughly scrub the mussels under cold running water with a small stiff brush and discard any that have damaged shells. Steam them open by placing them in a covered pan on a rack or steamer over simmering water for 5 minutes. Once cooked, remove the mussels from their shells. Discard any that have not opened.

2   Clean the squid and slice into 1 cm-thick rings. Plunge them into a pan of boiling water for no more than 1 minute and drain immediately. Do not overcook them or they will become tough.

3   If the prawns are uncooked, plunge them into the boiling water for 1 minute until they turn pink. Drain immediately, cool, then shell them.

4   Combine the cooked mussels, squid, prawns and chopped celery in a large mixing bowl and dress with the crushed garlic, olive oil, lemon juice and salt and pepper.

5   Divide the chopped lettuce into 4 portions and arrange on plates. Place the fish on top and garnish with plenty of chopped fresh parsley to serve.

PRAWN & MELON SALAD

This splendid combination of fresh prawns, juicy, sweet melon and lively flavourings (see above) makes a salad that is a perfect starter for an outdoor meal on a hot summer evening.

1   To cook the prawns, plunge them into boiling water for 1–2 minutes, then allow them to cool. Peel the prawns, leaving their tails on. Cut the melon in half and scoop out the flesh using a melon baller. Alternatively, cut the flesh into cubes. The best melons to use are those with firm flesh, such as Piel de Sapo. Place the melon pieces in a bowl with the cooked prawns and chopped celery.

2   Make the dressing – mix together the mayonnaise, lemon juice, curry powder, ginger and cayenne pepper. Stir well and pour over the prawns and melon. Mix thoroughly to ensure all the ingredients are evenly coated with the dressing. Allow to stand for at least 15–30 minutes, then divide into 4 portions and serve with snipped fresh chives if desired.

500 g prawns

1 yellow skinned or green skinned (Piel de Sapo) melon

2 sticks celery, chopped

125 ml ready-made mayonnaise

Juice of 1 lemon

1 tablespoon curry powder

1 teaspoon grated ginger

Pinch of cayenne pepper

Snipped fresh chives to garnish (optional)

Serves 4

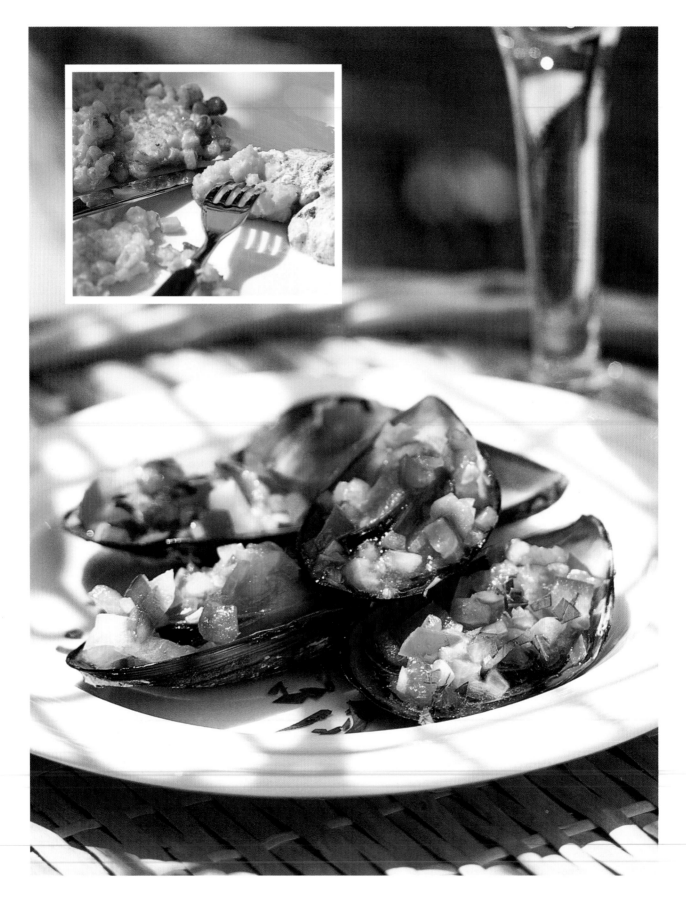

MUSSELS WITH SALSA

The salsa topping adds a splash of colour and additional flavour to these mussels, that are eaten directly from their shells (see left). They make an eye-catching appetiser for special occasions.

1　Scrub the mussels thoroughly under cold running water with a small, stiff brush and discard any that have damaged shells. Steam them open by placing them in a covered pan on a rack or steamer over simmering water for a few minutes. Remove the mussels from their shells and reserve 16 of the cleanest half-shells. Discard any mussels that have not opened.

2　For the salsa, finely chop the tomato, onion or shallots and the green pepper and place in a bowl. Pour the olive oil and lemon or lime juice over the chopped vegetables, then season with salt and pepper.

3　Mix the mussels with the salsa and allow to marinate in the refrigerator for at least 30 minutes.

4　When ready to serve, arrange the half-shells on a plate and, using a small spoon, place one mussel and a little salsa in each half-shell. Avoid placing too much liquid in the shells, as this may spill during serving and ruin the presentation. Sprinkle each filled shell with finely chopped fresh coriander or parsley – the green looks very attractive against the red salsa. The mussels should be eaten by hand, directly from the shell.

16 large mussels

1 small, firm tomato

1 small onion or 2 shallots, peeled

1 small green pepper

1 tablespoon olive oil

Juice of 1 lemon or 2 limes

Salt and pepper to taste

Finely chopped fresh coriander or parsley to garnish

Serves 4

SWEETCORN FRITTERS

Similar to small pancakes or blinis, sweetcorn fritters (see inset, left) make a good first course. Serve them hot with sun-dried tomato pesto mixed with crème fraîche. They are also delicious cold and are ideal for taking on picnics or serving with dips and drinks.

1　Beat the eggs in a bowl, then add the crème fraîche and continue beating until the two are thoroughly blended. Add the polenta flour (or maize meal) and mix well, making sure there are no lumps – if there are any lumps present, beat them out with a spoon. Once the mixture becomes a smooth batter, tip in the drained sweetcorn kernels and continue to mix.

2　Meanwhile, heat a little oil in a roomy, non-stick frying pan and drop a few tablespoons of the polenta, egg and crème fraîche mixture into the pan. Be careful not to overcrowd the pan – instead, cook the fritters in a few batches. Cook them for 2–3 minutes, then flip them over carefully and cook the other sides for a further 2–3 minutes. Drain on kitchen paper to absorb excess oil, then keep warm while cooking the rest. Allow roughly 2–3 fritters per portion. Serve with a generous dollop of crème fraîche mixed with sun-dried tomato pesto.

2 eggs

2 tablespoons crème fraîche

2 tablespoons fine polenta flour (or maize meal)

300 g cooked sweetcorn (canned is easiest)

Oil for frying

Crème fraîche and sun-dried tomato pesto to serve

Serves 4 (makes 12 fritters)

SPINACH ROULADE

FOR THE ROULADE

500 g cooked spinach, chopped
(1 kg fresh or frozen spinach)

5 eggs, separated

3 tablespoons single cream

Freshly grated nutmeg to taste

Salt and pepper to taste

FOR THE FILLING

200 g cream cheese

200 g crème fraîche

100 g smoked salmon trimmings

Black pepper to taste

Serves 8

Spinach roulade makes an impressive starter (see below) that is simple to prepare and keeps well for a day or two. Cook and drain the fresh spinach the day before it is needed if possible, to ensure it does not contain too much moisture. Frozen spinach can be used for this dish.

1   Preheat the oven to 200°C, gas mark 6. Grease a 25 x 36 cm swiss roll tin and line it with greaseproof paper, making sure the lining overshoots the edges of the tray a little.

2   Place the cooked and chopped spinach in a bowl. Make sure it is as dry as you feel is possible.

3   Mix the egg yolks, cream, nutmeg, salt and pepper into the spinach. Beat the egg whites until stiff, but not too dry and fold into the spinach mixture.

4   Spread the mixture evenly on to the lined swiss roll tin and place in the oven for 15 minutes. To check that the roulade is cooked, press it gently in the middle with your finger – if the sponge springs back into shape, it is cooked. If your finger leaves an impression, cook for a further 5 minutes.

5   Remove the tin from the oven and leave to stand for 5 minutes. Turn out on to a sheet of kitchen foil that is larger than the roulade and carefully peel off the greaseproof paper lining. It does not matter if a little of the spinach sticks to the paper.

6   To make the filling, mix the cream cheese and crème fraîche with the salmon trimmings and season with freshly ground black pepper.

7   While the spinach base is still warm, spread the cream cheese mixture on to it, gently roll up the roulade and wrap it in foil. Do not worry if the roll cracks a little, or if some of the filling squeezes out.

8   Allow the roulade to cool completely, then slice and serve. Sour cream or mayonnaise thinned into a runny sauce with some water – or a mixture of both – makes an excellent accompaniment.

MOULDED GAZPACHO

This dish is based on the traditional soup but without the bread and with gelatine added to help it take shape. Moulded gazpacho looks impressive set either in a large ring mould or in small oval dariole moulds for single portions.

1   Dissolve the gelatine in 3 tablespoons of very hot water in a small saucepan. (Always add the gelatine powder to the liquid, never the other way around.) Stir vigorously and allow to stand for 1–2 minutes, then, if not completely dissolved, place over very low heat for a few seconds and stir. Do not allow the liquid to boil. Once it is transparent and runny, allow to cool and add lemon juice to dilute further.

2   Place the tomatoes, pepper, shallots and garlic (if using) along with the vinegar and olive oil in a food processor. Process until everything is blended into a smooth and creamy mixture. Alternatively, pass the ingredients through a sieve and mix. Add the dissolved gelatine and stir again for a moment. Season with salt and pepper.

3   Transfer the gazpacho to a jug and wait until it begins to set. Stir from time to time to stop the mixture from separating. You should have approximately 1 litre of liquid.

4   As the gazpacho begins to set, pour it into an 800 ml ring mould or divide into 6 and pour into 150 ml oval dariole moulds. Chill for several hours.

5   When ready to serve, loosen the moulded gazpacho with a hot, sharp knife and turn out on to a large serving dish, or on to individual dishes if using smaller moulds. Serve with the chopped peppers and Saffron Mayonnaise (see page 19), which has been thinned with a little water.

1 tablespoon powdered gelatine (1 envelope)

4 very ripe tomatoes, medium-sized, peeled and deseeded

1 small green pepper, deseeded and chopped

2 shallots, peeled and chopped

1 clove garlic, peeled and crushed (optional)

2 tablespoons white wine vinegar

2 tablespoons olive oil

Salt and pepper to taste

Saffron Mayonnaise (see page 19) and a few chopped mixed peppers to serve

Serves 6

EGG & CUCUMBER TERRINE

This light terrine can be made in individual moulds or set in a loaf tin, then sliced. It makes an attractive first course, especially when decorated with a little cress or slices of cucumber (see right).

1 tablespoon powdered gelatine
(1 envelope)

250 g plain yogurt

2 tablespoons ready-made mayonnaise

Juice of 1 lemon

Salt and pepper to taste

Dash of Tabasco sauce

5 eggs, hard-boiled

1 large cucumber

Sliced cucumber to serve

Serves 6

1 Dissolve the gelatine in 3 tablespoons of very hot water in a small saucepan. (Always add the gelatine powder to the liquid, never the other way around.) Stir vigorously and allow to stand for 1–2 minutes, then, if not completely dissolved, place over very low heat for a few seconds and stir. Do not allow the liquid to boil. Once it is transparent and runny, allow it to cool and add lemon juice to dilute further.

2 Mix together the yogurt, mayonnaise and lemon juice and season with salt and pepper to taste. Add a dash of Tabasco sauce (taking care not to make the mixture too hot), then stir in the dissolved gelatine.

3 Peel and chop the hard-boiled eggs and dice the cucumber finely. Place these in a bowl and carefully fold in the liquid mixture.

4 Divide the terrine mixture into 6 and spoon into oiled 150 ml oval dariole moulds, or into an 800 ml loaf tin. Chill thoroughly for several hours.

5 Once the terrine has set, slide a sharp, heated knife around the edges of the terrine to loosen it from the mould. Turn out on to individual plates if using the dariole moulds, or on to a serving dish if using the loaf tin. Serve with the cucumber slices or a green salad.

CHICKEN LIVER PATE

Smooth and creamy chicken liver pâté always goes down well as a starter or lunch dish. Spread it thickly on freshly baked Herb and Olive Bread (see page 122).

50 g butter

1 small onion, peeled and chopped

1 clove garlic, peeled and chopped

250 g chicken livers

1 tablespoon chopped fresh thyme
(or mixed herbs)

1 tablespoon brandy

Freshly grated nutmeg to taste

Salt and pepper to taste

Oil or chopped fresh parsley to garnish

Serves 4–6

1 Melt the butter in a frying pan. Add the onion and garlic and cook gently until the onion is translucent. Chop up the livers, removing any veins and sinews. Add the chopped livers to the frying onions and garlic and cook together for 10 minutes until the livers are cooked through. Add the thyme and the brandy and cook for a further 1–2 minutes.

2 Place in a food processor (or a bowl, if using a hand-held blender). Grate a little nutmeg over the livers and season with salt and pepper, then process until smooth and creamy.

3 Spoon into a small terrine (or another suitable dish) and allow to cool. Cover the top of the pâté with a little oil to prevent it looking dry once it has cooled. Alternatively, cover the surface with chopped fresh parsley.

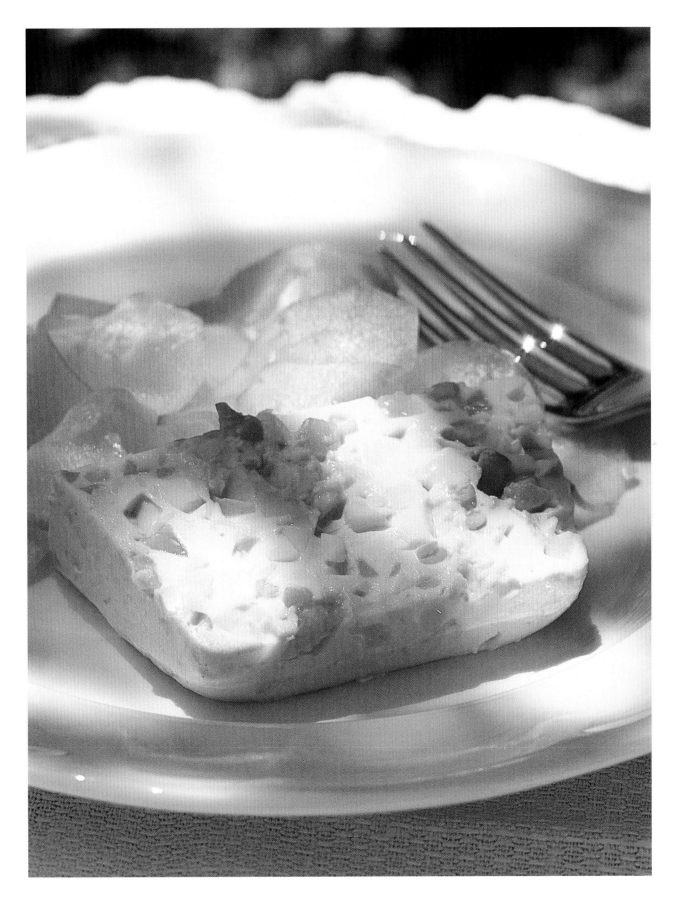

AVOCADO MOUSSE & PRAWN SAUCE

FOR THE MOUSSE

1 tablespoon powdered gelatine

2 large, very ripe avocados, peeled and roughly chopped

125 ml plain yogurt

125 ml ready-made mayonnaise

Juice of 1 lime

Salt if necessary

Tabasco sauce or cayenne pepper to taste

6 large prawns

Oil for greasing

FOR THE PRAWN SAUCE

250 g prawns, cooked and peeled

2 tablespoons ready-made mayonnaise

Juice of 1 lime

Salt and pepper to taste

Chopped fresh parsley to garnish

Serves 6

This light mousse, served with a creamy, flavoursome sauce makes an elegant first course. I like to set the mousse in six small moulds rather than one large one, as this makes for a neater presentation.

1 Dissolve the gelatine in 3 tablespoons of very hot water in a small pan. (Always add the gelatine powder to the liquid, never the other way around.) Stir vigorously and allow to stand for 1–2 minutes, then, if not completely dissolved, place over very low heat for a few seconds and stir. Do not allow the liquid to boil. Once it is transparent and runny, allow to cool and add lemon juice to dilute further.

2 Place the avocados, yogurt, mayonnaise, lime juice, salt and tabasco (or cayenne pepper) in a food processor and blend into a fine cream. Alternatively, place in a bowl and blend with a hand-held blender. Add the dissolved gelatine and mix well.

3 Place a large prawn on the base of each of the 150 ml individual moulds (oval dariole moulds or crème caramel moulds are ideal). Make sure you grease them lightly first. Pour in the avocado mixture and chill in the refrigerator for at least 2 hours, until set.

4 Meanwhile, make the prawn sauce. You do not need prawns of the best quality for this, as they will be puréed – properly thawed frozen prawns will be more than adequate. Place these in a food processor with the mayonnaise and lime juice, adding 1–2 tablespoons of water to dilute. Process until the sauce has the consistency of double cream. If you do not have a food processor, chop the prawns into very small pieces and mix them with the other ingredients using a hand whisk. Season with salt and pepper to taste.

5 Once the mousse has set, run a sharp, heated knife around the moulds and carefully turn out the mousses on to individual plates. To serve, pour some prawn sauce around each mousse and garnish with a sprinkling of chopped fresh parsley.

GUACAMOLE MOUSSE

Prepare the avocado mousse as instructed in step 2, above. Substitute the prawn sauce with a vegetable and vinaigrette dressing. Place half a diced cucumber, 1 diced red pepper, 1 peeled and finely chopped onion and 1 chopped tomato into a bowl and mix together well. Add 2 tablespoons of Vinaigrette (see page 91) and a sprinkling of chilli powder. Mix together until all the vegetables are thoroughly coated in the dressing. Garnish with a handful of chopped fresh coriander and place a large spoonful on each plate with the avocado mousse.

FISH MOUSSE

This mousse is very simple to make. Although smoked salmon (trimmings are more economical), smoked mackerel or smoked trout produce sublime results, any type of fish can be used – try a different variety each time to experiment. Unsmoked white fish may taste a little insipid, so a few anchovy fillets can be incorporated for added flavour.

1 tablespoon powdered gelatine (1 envelope)

400 g fish, cooked or smoked

Juice of 1 lemon

250 ml yogurt

2 tablespoons ready-made mayonnaise

Salt and black pepper to taste

1 tablespoon chopped fresh herbs such as parsley or tarragon (optional)

3 egg whites

Cucumber, thinly sliced, and watercress to serve

Serves 6

1 Dissolve the gelatine in 3 tablespoons of very hot water in a small saucepan. (Always add the gelatine powder to the liquid, never the other way around.) Stir vigorously and allow to stand for 1–2 minutes, then, if not completely dissolved, place over very low heat for a few seconds and stir. Do not allow the liquid to boil. Once it is transparent and runny, allow to cool and add a little lemon juice to dilute further.

2 Place the fish, the remaining lemon juice, yogurt, mayonnaise, salt (which may not be necessary if using smoked fish or anchovies) and black pepper in a food processor and combine until smooth. (Alternatively, blend the mixture in a bowl using a hand-held blender.) Add the cooled gelatine and mix well. If using a food processor, transfer the mixture into a bowl. Stir in the chopped fresh herbs.

3 Beat the egg whites in a separate bowl until stiff but not dry, then fold the beaten egg whites into the fish mixture gently, taking care not to beat the air out of them.

4 Divide the mousse into 6 portions and spoon each of these portions into an 150 ml oval dariole mould, or spoon the entire mixture into an 800 ml loaf tin. Chill in the refrigerator for several hours to set.

5 When ready to serve, slide a sharp, heated knife between the mousses and the moulds (or loaf tin) to loosen them. Turn out on to individual plates or a large serving dish and decorate with thinly sliced cucumber and bunches of watercress.

HAM MOUSSE

Prepare the gelatine as instructed in step 1, above. Mix 250 ml of yogurt with 2 tablespoons of ready-made mayonnaise and 2 tablespoons of gluten-free Dijon mustard in a bowl. Add the dissolved gelatine. Mix well, then mix in 400 g of cooked minced ham and season with salt and pepper to taste. (Ham tends to be fairly salty, so it may not be necessary to add salt.) For a light mousse, fold in 2 stiffly beaten egg whites. For a more solid, terrine-like texture, omit the egg whites.

Thinly slice 3–4 gherkins lengthways and arrange the slices on the base of an 800 ml loaf tin. Spoon the ham mixture over the top of the gherkins and chill for at least 2 hours before serving. Slide a sharp, heated knife between the terrine and the mould and carefully turn out on to a plate. Decorate with a few gherkins and serve.

2
Lunches & Suppers

FISH

POULTRY

MEAT

CHEESE & EGGS

RICE

POLENTA

PULSES

Baked Cod with Tomatoes

The crisp, sunny taste of fresh tomatoes is the essence of this dish (see left). As with any tomato recipe the quality of the fruit is paramount. If good tomatoes cannot be obtained, a simple tomato sauce may be used, but the recipe will not retain the freshness that brings it to life.

Oil for greasing

500 g ripe tomatoes

2 tablespoons olive oil

1 large onion, peeled and chopped

2 cloves garlic, peeled and chopped

1 bay leaf

1 teaspoon dried oregano

Salt and black pepper to taste

800 g cod fillet (or fillets)

2 eggs, hard-boiled, chopped

Handful of chopped fresh parsley to garnish

Serves 4

1   Preheat the oven to 180°C, gas mark 4. Grease a 20 x 30 cm gratin dish with oil. To peel the tomatoes, make a small incision in the skin of each one, then plunge them into boiling water for 1 minute. Lift them out of the hot water using a slotted spoon and plunge them into cold water immediately. Allow them to sit in the cold water for approximately 1 minute, then remove. The skins should now come away from the flesh easily. Roughly chop the peeled tomatoes.

2   Heat 2 tablespoons of olive oil in a saucepan over medium heat and soften the onion and garlic in the oil. Once translucent, not brown, add the tomatoes, then the bay leaf and dried oregano. Season with salt and pepper to taste. Slowly bring the mixture to a boil and allow to simmer for no more than 5 minutes, so the tomatoes are not reduced to a pulp, but remain fairly chunky.

3   Cut the cod fillet or fillets into suitable sizes for individual portions, each weighing roughly 200 g. Place these in the oiled gratin dish and season with salt and pepper.

4   Pour the hot tomato stew over the pieces of cod and bake in the preheated oven for 15–20 minutes, until the fish is tender and the sauce is bubbling. Garnish with chopped hard-boiled eggs and chopped fresh parsley and serve with boiled new potatoes and a green salad.

BAKED HALIBUT OR TURBOT STEAKS
Other filleted fish such as haddock or coley can be used in the same way as the cod fillets in the recipe above. However, fish steaks such as halibut or turbot, although a little extravagant, can also be used just as successfully. These should be cooked a little longer, for about 30 minutes.

BAKED FISH PARCELS
Fillets of cod, haddock and coley, or steaks of halibut and turbot can be baked in parcels to retain their flavour and moisture. Make a paste in a mortar using a pestle by grinding together 4 tablespoons of olive oil, 2 chopped shallots and 4 tablespoons of chopped mixed herbs such as parsley, dill and basil. Add a little salt and freshly ground black pepper to taste. Cut 4 sheets·of kitchen foil or parchment to a size that is slightly larger than that of the fish and place a fillet or steak on each sheet. Cover the fish with the herb paste and wrap it up in the foil carefully, tucking in the ends. Place the parcels on an oiled baking tray and bake in a preheated oven for 20–30 minutes (depending on the fish) at 200°C, gas mark 4. Serve in their parcels with lemon wedges.

FISH PIE

This dish is best when made with a variety of fish and shellfish. Smoked haddock gives the sauce additional flavour and prawns add a lively splash of colour. Include some hard-boiled eggs and top the dish with mashed potato to give it texture and body. Fish pie is a family favourite which is both nutritious and filling.

1 Preheat the oven to 200°C, gas mark 6. Grease a 1.5 litre ovenproof pie dish with melted butter.

2 Wash and peel the potatoes, then cut them into pieces. Place in a saucepan and cover with water. Add salt and bring to a boil. Reduce the heat and simmer for 15–20 minutes until the potatoes are soft, then drain well. Mash the potatoes in the saucepan with the butter and milk until smooth, adding salt and pepper to taste. Meanwhile, place the eggs in a small saucepan of water and bring to a boil. Reduce the heat and simmer for 6 minutes until nearly hard-boiled, then allow to cool.

3 Place the cod and haddock in a saucepan with the milk, bay leaf, onion and peppercorns. Bring the mixture to a boil, then remove from the heat. Cover the pan and leave to stand in a warm place for 10 minutes to allow the fish to cook through and the milk to be infused with the flavour of the fish, creating a deliciously aromatic liquid for the sauce. Remove the fish with a slotted spoon and set aside to cool. Strain the cooking liquid and reserve.

4 Make a white sauce – dissolve the cornflour in 2 tablespoons of cold milk and stir into the hot infused milk. Slowly bring the liquid to a boil, stirring continuously, then simmer for 1 minute before adding the lemon juice. Remove the sauce from the heat and set aside. It should have a fairly thick consistency.

5 Flake the cooked fish, carefully removing any skin and bones. Place the flakes in the white sauce and add the cooked prawns. Season with salt and pepper and add a little grated nutmeg and dill, if desired. Gently fold the fish into the sauce until thoroughly mixed.

6 Shell the boiled eggs and cut in half. Lay the halved eggs on the base of the greased pie dish, then spoon the fish mixture over the top. Cover the fish with a layer of mashed potato and decorate the top surface with wavy fork marks. Bake in the preheated oven for 30 minutes until the potato topping is brown and the sauce is bubbling. Serve immediately with a green salad or a vegetable side dish.

Butter for greasing

600 g potatoes

Pinch of salt

25 g butter and 100 ml milk for mashing potatoes

Salt and white pepper to taste

2 eggs, medium-sized

250 g cod fillet

250 g smoked haddock

1 litre milk

1 bay leaf

1 small onion, peeled and chopped

A few black peppercorns

50 g cornflour

2 tablespoons cold milk

Juice of 1 lemon

100 g prawns, peeled and cooked

Freshly grated nutmeg to taste (optional)

Chopped fresh dill to taste (optional)

Serves 4

CRUNCHY CRUMBLE TOPPING

Replace the potato topping with a crunchy crumble topping: blend 150 g of maize meal, 90 g of butter, 1 tablespoon of freshly grated Parmesan and some chopped fresh parsley. Sprinkle over the fish mixture and bake as above.

CHICKEN WITH BASIL & ALMONDS

Succulent chicken breasts are accompanied in this dish by a vibrant green basil sauce, thickened with ground almonds and sour cream, with garlic and lemon juice for added flavour. This nourishing supper can be made very quickly and easily.

4 chicken breasts, skinned

2 tablespoons olive oil

100 g ground almonds

2 cloves garlic, peeled and crushed

50 g finely shredded fresh basil, plus extra to garnish

Juice of 1 lemon

300 ml sour cream

Salt and pepper to taste

Serves 4

1 Gently poach the chicken breasts in 2–3 tablespoons of water with the oil for 10 minutes on each side. Try not to brown them.

2 Meanwhile, make the sauce – mix the ground almonds, garlic, basil, lemon juice and sour cream into a smooth sauce, in a food processor, or with a wooden spoon in a bowl. Season with salt and pepper.

3 Once the chicken breasts are almost cooked, pour in the sauce, mixing it with the juices in the pan. Cook for a further 10 minutes until the sauce has heated through. Garnish with shredded fresh basil and serve with brown rice or boiled potatoes.

CHICKEN, AVOCADO & YOGURT MAYONNAISE

This lunch dish is ideal for scorching hot days, which is often the case in the Spanish summer. The spicy, slightly tangy mayonnaise is both light and refreshing and works well with cold chicken. Serve with Spicy Moroccan Rice (see page 68).

FOR THE CHICKEN

1 cold cooked chicken (roasted or poached), medium-sized

2 ripe avocados

Chopped fresh coriander to garnish

FOR THE YOGURT MAYONNAISE

200 ml plain yogurt

100 ml ready-made mayonnaise

Juice of 1 lemon

1 tablespoon curry powder

1 teaspoon ground coriander

Salt and black pepper to taste

Serves 4

1 Remove the skin from the chicken and discard. Separate the flesh from the bones and cut it into bite-sized pieces. Place the pieces in a large bowl.

2 To make the sauce, mix the yogurt with the mayonnaise, lemon juice, curry powder and ground coriander and beat until smooth. Leave to stand for at least half an hour to allow the sauce to be infused by the spices.

3 Pour the sauce into the bowl with the chicken pieces and mix well to cover all the pieces of chicken thoroughly in sauce. Add salt and freshly ground black pepper to taste.

4 Cut the avocados into quarters lengthways, then into eighths, removing the skin as you go. Wet the flesh with lemon juice to stop it discolouring.

5 To serve, place the sauce in a large shallow serving dish and sit the chicken in the sauce. Arrange the avocado wedges around the chicken. Sprinkle the entire dish liberally with chopped coriander.

CHICKEN FRIED WITH ROSEMARY & GARLIC

In this simple recipe the chicken pieces are cooked in garlic and fresh rosemary (see above) – a light and tasty combination that is good hot or cold. This dish is ideal for picnics.

1   Season the pieces of chicken with salt and pepper to taste. Heat the oil in a heavy-based frying pan over medium heat and fry the chicken pieces in the oil for approximately 15 minutes until fairly brown and crispy. Make sure you turn them from time to time so that they are evenly cooked and browned all over.

2   Add the garlic and rosemary to the pan and continue to fry for a further 10–15 minutes. Remove from the pan and serve immediately with sautéed potatoes and vegetables, or allow to cool and serve cold as part of a picnic or summer lunch with Pesto Rice (see page 59) and a dressed green salad.

1 chicken, medium-sized, jointed into 8 pieces (thighs or legs)

Salt and pepper to taste

2 tablespoons olive oil

6 cloves garlic, peeled and sliced

Handful of chopped fresh rosemary leaves

Serves 4

Chicory & Ham Gratin

4 chicory heads, cut in half horizontally

Knob of butter

8 slices smoked ham

300 ml Cheese Sauce (see page 91)

25 g freshly grated Parmesan cheese

Serves 4

The bitter taste of chicory, also known as Belgian endive, adds a pungency to this ham and cheese gratin.

1 Preheat the oven to 220°C, gas mark 7. Trim the chicory and place it in a large saucepan that has a lid with the butter and 2–3 tablespoons of water. Cover the pan and cook over low heat for 20 minutes, turning once, until tender. Add more water as necessary. Once cooked, allow to cool slightly.

2 Lay the slices of ham on a chopping board and place a piece of cooled chicory on each slice. Wrap the ham around each chicory head.

3 Arrange the wrapped chicory and ham pieces in a deep ovenproof dish and pour over the cheese sauce. Sprinkle with the Parmesan cheese.

4 Bake in the top half of the preheated oven for 20–30 minutes, until the cheese topping is golden brown and the chicory heads are tender. Serve immediately, with boiled new potatoes or baked potatoes, if desired.

Beef Pie with Olives & Raisins

2 tablespoons olive oil

500 g minced beef

1 small onion, peeled and chopped

1 carrot, medium-sized, chopped

1 tablespoon cornflour

300 ml beef stock

1 tablespoon tomato purée

1 teaspoon dried, mixed herbs

Salt and black pepper to taste

25 pitted green olives

50 g seedless raisins

Mashed Potatoes (see page 72)

Serves 4–6

This is a gluten-free version of the popular English favourite, Cottage Pie, a delicious hot dish of flavoured minced meat topped with mashed potatoes. Here, green olives and raisins are added to the minced beef which gives this dish an exotic twist.

1 Preheat the oven to 200°C, gas mark 6. Heat the oil in a frying pan and add the minced beef. Cook over high heat for 5 minutes, stirring occasionally, until the meat is evenly browned.

2 Stir the chopped onion and carrot into the pan with the meat and cook for a further 10 minutes. Sprinkle the cornflour into the pan and stir well to combine with the meat and vegetables.

3 Pour in the beef stock, add the tomato purée and mixed herbs and season with salt and black pepper. Stir the mixture again, then bring to a boil. Reduce the heat and simmer covered for 30 minutes, stirring occasionally until the meat is cooked through and the sauce has thickened. Finally stir in the olives and raisins.

4 Spoon the cooked meat mixture into a 20 x 30 cm ovenproof dish and cover with the mashed potatoes. Decorate the top surface with fork marks. Bake at the top of the preheated oven for 25–30 minutes until the potato topping is brown. Serve piping hot with a green vegetable.

BEEF SALAD WITH MUSTARD DRESSING

Cold cooked beef is mixed with gherkins and shallots and tossed in a mustard and red wine vinegar dressing for a dramatic blend of flavours. This salad is ideal for using up cooked leftover meat, but if you do not have any, use grilled steak meat or ham as an alternative.

1 Cut the beef into strips of about 5 x 1 cm. Place them in a large mixing bowl with the chopped gherkins and shallots.

2 To make the dressing, place the oil, vinegar, mustard, sugar and garlic in a separate bowl. Blend with a whisk or hand-held blender until the mustard is combined with the oil and vinegar and the dressing is smooth. If it is too thick, add a tablespoon of cold water.

3 Pour the dressing over the beef and stir. Add salt and pepper to taste (salt may not be necessary as the mustard can be quite salty). Leave to stand for at least 30 minutes before serving to allow the meat to absorb the flavour of the mustard. Garnish with chives and serve with a crispy green salad.

600 g cold cooked beef

2 tablespoons gherkins, chopped

2 shallots, peeled and chopped

150 ml vegetable or olive oil

5 teaspoons red wine vinegar

2 tablespoons gluten-free Dijon mustard

½ teaspoon sugar

1 clove garlic, peeled and crushed

Salt and pepper to taste

Snipped fresh chives to garnish

Serves 4

PORK WITH TUNA & YOGURT SAUCE

This cold dish of tender pork slices topped with a creamy tuna and anchovy sauce is my version of the classic Italian dish 'Vitello tonnato' which is based on veal. I prefer to use pork as I feel it has more flavour and I use yogurt in place of cream in the sauce for a lighter result.

1 Preheat the oven to 200°C, gas mark 6. Wrap the pork loin in foil and place in a roasting tin surrounded with a little water. Roast in the preheated oven for 60–85 minutes until cooked through but not dry. To check the joint is cooked, pierce it with a sharp knife through to the middle and if the juices run clear, the meat is cooked. Remove the pork loin from the oven and allow to cool, keeping it wrapped in the foil to ensure it does not dry out.

2 To prepare the tuna sauce, place the tuna fish (and its oil) in a mixing bowl with the anchovies, yogurt, mayonnaise and lemon juice. Season with black pepper to taste, but not with salt as the fish is salty enough. Blend the mixture with a hand-held blender or in a mortar with a pestle until it has the consistency of double cream.

3 When ready to serve carve the cold meat into thin slices and arrange on a serving plate. Pour the sauce over the meat and scatter the capers on the top. Serve with cold Lentil and Grilled Pepper Salad (see page 48).

FOR THE PORK

1 kg pork loin, off the bone

FOR THE TUNA SAUCE

100 g canned tuna fish in oil

2 anchovy fillets

125 ml plain yogurt

1 tablespoon ready-made mayonnaise

Juice of ½ lemon

Black pepper to taste

2 tablespoons capers to garnish

Serves 6

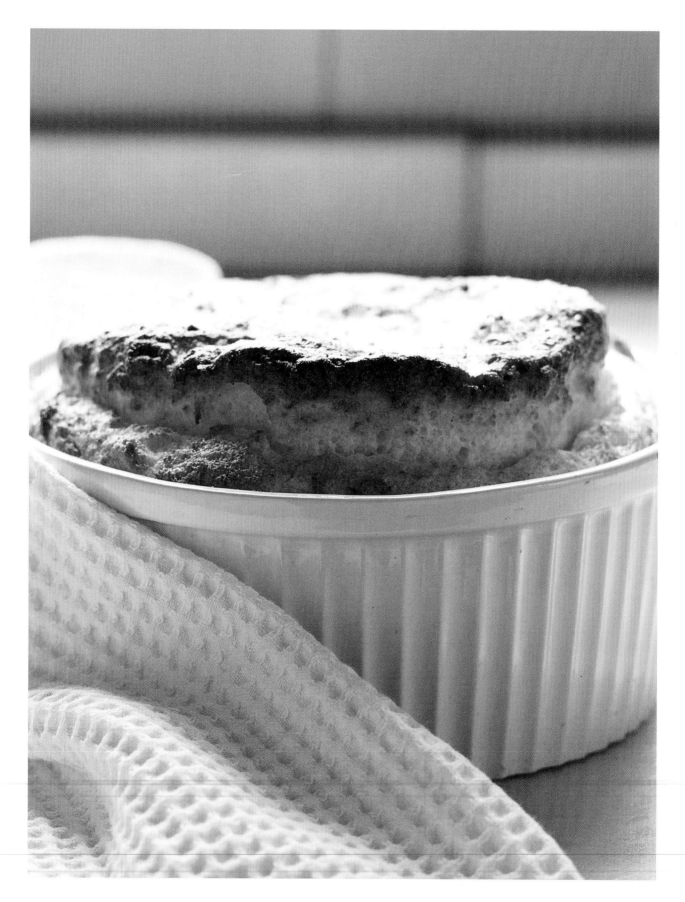

SOUFFLE

This basic soufflé recipe is an excellent example of how successfully maize meal (or cornmeal) can be used as a substitute for wheat flour. No matter how simple, a soufflé is always impressive, but there are many interesting possibilities when it comes to selecting flavourings. Make sure your sauce is thick initially, and then lightened by the stiffly beaten egg whites. This produces a well risen soufflé that makes an ideal first course or lunch dish.

25 g butter, plus extra for greasing

25 g maize meal (or cornmeal)

250 ml milk

4 eggs, medium-sized, separated

100 g flavouring such as grated cheddar cheese, fish or puréed vegetables

Seasonings, such as salt and pepper to taste and a pinch of freshly grated nutmeg or a herb, where appropriate

1 tablespoon freshly grated Parmesan cheese or 1 tablespoon polenta

Serves 4

1   Preheat the oven to 200°C, gas mark 6. Grease a 1.5 litre soufflé dish with a little melted butter. Melt the remaining butter in a large pan and stir in the maize meal. Cook for 1–2 minutes. Gradually pour in the milk, stirring continuously until it is blended smoothly with the maize meal. Simmer for 3 minutes, stirring constantly – this prevents lumps from forming in the sauce. Set aside to allow the mixture to cool slightly.

2   Mix in the egg yolks, the flavouring (see below) and seasonings. Make sure you select seasonings that work well with your chosen flavouring. For instance, nutmeg works well with the flavours of cheese and smoked fish, and herbs such as parsley go well with puréed vegetables. Salt and pepper work well with most flavours.

3   Beat the egg whites (which should be at room temperature) until stiff and dry. Fold a little of the beaten egg whites into the sauce, then carefully fold in the rest. Take care not to knock the air out of the egg whites as you mix them in, as it is the air that causes the soufflé to rise and gives it the light, airy texture it is known for.

4   Sprinkle either the freshly grated Parmesan cheese or polenta into the base of the greased dish – this keeps the soufflé mixture stuck to the sides of the dish as it cooks, which helps it to rise. Pour in the soufflé mixture. Bake in the preheated oven for 35–40 minutes – make sure the soufflé does not overcook and become dry. Wobble the dish carefully to check whether or not the centre is set. Serve immediately.

FLAVOURINGS

If using cheese or fish, use strongly flavoured varieties. Mature cheddar is best for cheese soufflés – it should be grated and added to the basic sauce. Smoked salmon or smoked haddock are good fish choices. Poach the fish, then mash it with a fork and add to the basic sauce.

To add a lively hint of colour, spinach or watercress can be used. The leaves should first be wilted, then broken down in a food processor or mashed with a fork before being added to the basic sauce. If using vegetables with a delicate flavour, add some cheese, such as freshly grated Parmesan. Broccoli is also a delicious vegetable for using in soufflés. Steam the broccoli florets for 2–3 minutes until just tender, then rinse in cold water and chop finely. Add to the basic sauce with some chopped, fried shallots and crumbled blue cheese.

CHEESE & ONION TART

The classic combination of cheese and onion always works a treat. In my gluten-free version of this tart, maize meal is used to make a pastry case, which is baked blind before being filled and baked again.

FOR THE SHORTCRUST PASTRY CASE

150 g maize meal (or cornmeal)

50 g butter, chilled and cut into small pieces

1 egg, medium-sized, beaten

Pinch of salt (if the butter is unsalted)

FOR THE CHEESE & ONION FILLING

4 eggs, medium-sized

100 g double cream or plain yogurt

100 g mature cheddar or blue cheese, grated

Pepper to taste

Freshly grated nutmeg to taste

1 onion, medium-sized, peeled and thinly sliced

A knob of butter

Serves 4–6

1 Preheat the oven to 180°C, gas mark 4. Blend the maize meal and butter, either in a food processor or by crumbling the butter into the flour with your fingers until the mixture resembles breadcrumbs. Once the maize meal and butter are well blended, mix in the salt (if using).

2 Add the beaten egg to the mixture to make a dough. If the pastry is too dry and crumbly, add a drop or two of water to help it bind together. Shape the dough into a ball with your hands.

3 Place the pastry ball between two sheets of clingfilm and flatten it with the base of your palm. Roll it out into a fairly even sheet of pastry large enough to line a 25 cm flan tin. Remove the top sheet of clingfilm and, using the lower sheet, lift up the pastry and turn it over on to the flan tin. Remove the clingfilm and press the pastry into the tin, working it across the base and up the sides. Cut off excess pastry and use it to patch up broken or thin areas. Handle the pastry as little as possible. If using 12 cm tartlet tins for individual servings, line as many as you can, then shape the leftover pastry into a new ball. Re-roll this between clingfilm and use to line the remaining tins.

4 Place the tin (or tins) on a baking sheet in the preheated oven. Bake for approximately 15 minutes.

5 Meanwhile, make the filling – blend the eggs, cream (or yogurt) and grated cheese together in a food processor, or mix them thoroughly in a bowl using a hand whisk. Add the pepper and grated nutmeg. (Salt will not be necessary as the cheese is salty enough.)

6 Remove the pastry shell from the oven and set aside to cool slightly. Meanwhile, melt the butter in a frying pan and fry the sliced onion until softened, but not browned. Place in the part-cooked pastry case (or cases).

7 Pour the egg mixture on to the onions and place on a baking tray. Bake in the preheated oven for 30 minutes if using a large tin, or 20 minutes if using small tartlet tins. In either case, ensure the filling is cooked in the middle before removing from the oven. Allow to cool a little before serving, or serve cold, with a mixed salad.

BACON AND CHEESE TART
Replace the onions with 50 g of smoked bacon, cut into cubes, and fry in a little oil over high heat for 2–3 minutes until cooked, but not crispy. Scatter these over the pastry shell, then pour in the filling and bake as above.

TORTILLA

This substantial omelette – known in Spain as the 'Tortilla' – is a vital part of the traditional Spanish tapas (see above). Warm, freshly cooked tortilla is delicious on its own or with grilled meat and fish. Slices of cold tortilla, served with a green salad, make excellent picnic fare.

1   Gently fry the potatoes and the onion (if using) in 3 tablespoons of the oil in a large non-stick frying pan for 20 minutes, until the potatoes start to break up. Avoid browning or burning them.

2   Whisk the eggs in a bowl and season with salt and pepper. Transfer the cooked potatoes – while still hot – to the bowl containing the eggs and mix well, ensuring the potatoes are thoroughly coated with the egg mixture. (The trick with making a proper tortilla is to place the hot potatoes into the eggs, not vice versa.)

3   Heat the remaining oil in a smaller (20 cm) non-stick frying pan and spread the mixture evenly over the base by gently shaking the pan. (The eggs and potatoes are, traditionally, placed back into the original frying pan, but the method given here results in a thicker, more moist omelette.)

4   Gently cook the tortilla over low heat for 10 minutes. Once the first side is browned, place a plate over the tortilla and then turn the frying pan upside-down, then slide the tortilla back into the frying pan with the cooked-side facing up. Or cook the second side under a hot grill, but ensure the omelette does not burn. Allow to cool a little before serving.

| 450 g potatoes, peeled and sliced |
| 1 onion, peeled and chopped (optional) |
| 4 tablespoons olive oil |
| 4 large eggs |
| Salt and pepper to taste |
| Serves 4 |

RISOTTO

This basic risotto can accompany grilled meat or fish dishes or may be served on its own as a main course, sprinkled with plenty of grated Parmesan. Vegetables, cooked with the rice, add colour and texture. Risotto is only as good as its stock – make sure it has a strong flavour.

1 Heat the butter and/or oil in a saucepan and cook the onion and garlic until the onion is translucent, not brown. Add the rice and stir until the grains are thoroughly coated and become slightly translucent. Add the wine and heat until the rice has absorbed the liquid.

2 Pour in the hot stock, stir and bring slowly to a boil. Reduce the heat and simmer uncovered, stirring occasionally for 18–20 minutes, until the liquid is absorbed and the rice is *al dente*, or firm to bite. Risotto should be creamy in texture, so add a little more stock if necessary.

3 Mix in half the grated Parmesan cheese and season with freshly ground black pepper. (Salt is probably unnecessary as the cheese is quite salty.) Sprinkle the remaining cheese over the risotto and serve immediately.

---

50 g butter or 2 tablespoons olive oil (or an equal mixture of both)

1 small onion, peeled and chopped

1 clove garlic, peeled and chopped

300 g risotto rice such as Arborio or Carnaroli

125 ml dry white wine

900 ml hot chicken or vegetable stock

50 g freshly grated Parmesan cheese

Black pepper to taste

Serves 4 (or 6 as a side dish)

CHOOSING THE RIGHT RICE

Rice is versatile – it absorbs flavours and can be served as a meal in itself or as an accompaniment to many dishes. It is a good staple in a gluten-free diet. Of the many types of rice, two are most widely used in cooking – long-grain and short-grain. Long-grain rice is good either boiled or steamed, plain or flavoured. For the recipes here, use Basmati rice or any variety of American long-grain rice. Short-grain rice absorbs moisture but does not become soggy, hence is used for risottos. It is coated in heated oil or butter before the cooking liquid is added. The Italian Arborio rice is best for risottos and the Spanish Valencian variety is my choice for paellas. Any short-grain rice may be used for the recipes here. Brown rice, either long- or short-grain, is unpolished rice, so is rich in fibre. It is slow to cook and does not absorb flavours as much as polished varieties. I do not recommend precooked or instant rices.

COOKING LONG-GRAIN RICE

For 4 servings, use 200 g of rice, 400 ml of water and salt to taste. Wash and drain the rice and place in a saucepan with the water and salt. Bring to a boil, then simmer covered for exactly 10 minutes from the start of boiling. Remove from the heat and fluff with a fork – the liquid should be absorbed. Cover and leave to stand for 2–3 minutes before serving.

FLAVOURING LONG-GRAIN RICE

To enhance plain boiled rice: use stock instead of water for a rich flavour; add a bay leaf and a knob of butter to the cooking water for fragrant rice; for a dramatic colour and a wonderfully musty flavour, add a pinch of saffron; add a couple of segment-sized pieces of orange peel to the cooking water for tangy, perfumed rice – sprinkle with slivers of toasted almonds to serve.

Risotto Croquettes

These fried risotto patties (see inset, right) are delicious served with fresh Tomato Sauce (see page 55). Serve them hot as a starter, or cold as a snack or as part of a picnic. Allow 2–3 croquettes per person.

3 eggs

1 kg cooked cold Risotto (see page 43)

3 tablespoons maize meal (optional)

Handful of chopped fresh parsley

Oil for frying

Makes approximately 12 croquettes

1 Beat the eggs and mix them into the cold risotto. Add the maize meal (which helps to bind the grains of rice together) and the chopped fresh parsley. Mix thoroughly using a fork.

2 Divide the mixture into 12 portions and shape each into an 8 cm long patty, roughly 1.5 cm thick. Heat the oil in a heavy-based frying pan and add the patties. Fry them over medium heat for approximately 5 minutes until crisp and brown underneath. Turn the patties carefully and fry the other sides for a further 5 minutes. Drain on a sheet of kitchen paper and serve either immediately with Tomato Sauce (see page 55) or ketchup, or allow to cool and serve as a snack.

Asparagus Risotto

A hint of saffron and a few asparagus spears transforms a basic risotto into this bright and colourful dish (see right).

2 tablespoons olive oil

1 small onion, peeled and chopped

1 clove garlic, peeled and chopped

125 g thin asparagus spears, stems trimmed

300 g risotto rice

125 ml dry white wine

Generous pinch of saffron strands, dried and powdered (see page 19)

900 ml chicken or vegetable stock

Salt and pepper to taste

Serves 4 (or 6 as a side dish)

1 Heat the oil in a medium-sized saucepan. Add the onion and garlic and cook gently until soft. Chop the asparagus stalks. Reserve the tips and add the stalks to the pan. Fry with the onion and garlic for 1–2 minutes, then add the rice. Stir until the grains are fully coated in the oil and are slightly translucent. Add the wine and reduce over high heat until the rice has absorbed the liquid.

2 Dissolve the dried and powdered saffron (see page 19) in the hot stock and add this to the rice. Stir the mixture and bring to a boil, then reduce the heat and simmer uncovered for 10 minutes, stirring occasionally. Add the asparagus tips and cook for a further 8–10 minutes. The rice is cooked when the liquid is absorbed and the rice is creamy and *al dente*, or firm to bite. Add salt and pepper to taste and remove from the heat. Serve immediately.

MUSHROOM RISOTTO

To make a mushroom risotto, substitute the asparagus with 25 g of dried mushrooms soaked in 100 ml of hot water. Add the mushrooms to the onions, garlic and rice in the saucepan and pour over the hot stock and mushroom water (instead of the wine). Cook as for Asparagus Risotto, above, omitting the saffron. Once the rice is cooked, stir in a pinch of freshly ground nutmeg, salt and pepper and serve with a topping made from 25 g of freshly grated Parmesan cheese.

POLENTA

1 litre water

1 teaspoon salt

200 g polenta (or maize meal)

Black pepper to taste

Freshly grated nutmeg to taste (optional)

Makes 8 slices (400 g)

Used widely in Northern Italian cooking, polenta is a gluten-free Godsend. It has endless possibilities and makes a good substitute for rice or potatoes. Bear in mind that its strength is its texture, so serve it with a strong-tasting ingredient or spicy sauce. The recipe that follows is for standard polenta, but you can buy instant polenta which is just as good and easier to cook – just follow the packet instructions.

1 Place the water in a large saucepan, add the salt and bring to a boil. Then pour the polenta gradually into the boiling water, stirring constantly.

2 Reduce the heat and simmer for 30 minutes, stirring constantly to avoid burning. When it has a thick consistency and pulls away from the sides of the pan easily, remove the polenta from the heat, season with black pepper and nutmeg, if desired. Either use immediately or spoon into a 1 litre loaf tin, allow to cool, then turn out and slice.

INSTANT, READY-TO-USE POLENTA

Instant polenta and ready-to-eat polenta (which comes vacuum packed) are both easy alternatives to making your own polenta and are just as good. Both are available from leading supermarkets. Follow the packet instructions.

POLENTA CROUTONS

Cut polenta slices into small dice and deep-fry them in vegetable oil until crispy. Drain on kitchen paper and use in thick soups and salads.

POLENTA AU GRATIN

Place prepared slices of polenta in a deep flameproof dish, cover with fresh Tomato Sauce (see page 55), sprinkle liberally with cheese and grill until the cheese bubbles (see right). Alternatively, top the slices with sautéed vegetables such as mushrooms and aubergines or with leftover ratatouille, sprinkle with freshly grated Parmesan cheese and grill. Try placing strips of grilled peppers and anchovy fillets on grilled slices of polenta and drizzle with olive oil.

POLENTA GNOCCHI

Gnocchi is an Italian dish that is usually based on potato, but polenta offers a delicious alternative. This version is very simple to prepare.

Oil for greasing
1 litre milk
1 large onion, peeled and studded with 1–2 cloves
1 bay leaf
Freshly grated nutmeg to taste
Pinch of salt
150 g polenta or coarse maize meal
3 egg yolks
100 g freshly grated Parmesan cheese
Freshly ground black pepper to taste
Butter for greasing
Serves 4 (makes 400 g)

1   Lightly grease a baking tray with a little oil. Pour the milk into a large saucepan, add the onion and bay leaf, a little grated nutmeg and the salt. Bring to a boil, then reduce the heat to a low setting and simmer gently for at least 10 minutes. Remove the onion and bay leaf from the pan with a slotted spoon and discard.

2   Hold the bag containing the polenta high above the pan and pour into the hot milk in a slow, steady stream, stirring constantly. Continue stirring and cook the mixture over low heat for 10 minutes or until it has a thick consistency and pulls away from the sides of the pan. Add some more milk if the polenta becomes too thick.

3   Remove from the heat and beat in the egg yolks, one at a time. Beat in half the grated Parmesan cheese and season with salt, lots of freshly ground black pepper and a little more grated nutmeg if desired.

4   Turn the polenta out on to the baking tray and spread into an even layer, roughly 1 cm thick. Brush with melted butter, then leave to cool and set for at least 20 minutes. Meanwhile, preheat the oven to 230°C, gas mark 8. Grease an ovenproof dish with melted butter.

5   When set, cut the polenta into 5 cm squares and place them, overlapping, in the ovenproof dish. Sprinkle the remaining Parmesan cheese over the gnocchi and bake in the top of the oven for roughly 15 minutes, until nicely browned. Serve with a salad tossed in a herb and garlic dressing.

LENTIL & GRILLED PEPPER SALAD

250 g Puy lentils

3 peppers: I red, I green and I yellow, deseeded

I large onion, peeled

I tablespoon oil

Salt and pepper to taste

Balsamic Vinaigrette (see below)

Handful of chopped fresh parsley to garnish

Serves 4–5

This attractive and substantial salad (see above) is delicious either cold or warm. Mixed chargrilled peppers add colour and a strong flavour, which is intensified by the onions and Balsamic Vinaigrette.

1 Cook the lentils in plenty of boiling water for 20 minutes, until tender, then drain. Meanwhile, dice the peppers and onion, toss them in warmed oil and grill until the edges become a little charred – do not cook through.

2 Mix the grilled peppers and onion with the cooked warm lentils, season with salt and pepper and dress with Balsamic Vinaigrette (see below). Sprinkle with chopped fresh parsley and serve immediately.

TO MAKE BALSAMIC VINAIGRETTE
Place 4 parts of extra virgin olive oil, 1 part of balsamic vinegar, 1 clove of garlic, cut in half or, for stronger flavour, crushed, 1 teaspoon of mustard and salt and pepper in a jar with a lid and shake well. Adjust the seasoning to taste.

LENTIL & BACON STEW

Robust and spicy, this stew can be cooked in advance and successfully reheated, making it an ideal winter supper dish. Any variety of lentils can be used and they do not need to be soaked beforehand.

1 Chop the bacon into 1 cm pieces. Heat the oil in a heavy-based casserole that has a lid and gently fry the bacon with the onion for 2–3 minutes. Add the crushed garlic, carrot, chilli and ground coriander and continue to cook for a further 2–3 minutes.

2 Meanwhile, rinse and drain the lentils. Place them into the casserole with the vegetables and flavourings and stir well to coat the lentils thoroughly with the mixture. Add the canned tomatoes with all the liquid from the can, then add the water and a pinch of salt.

3 Slowly bring the mixture to a boil, then reduce the heat and simmer covered for 40 minutes, until the lentils are soft. If the lentils become a little too dry, add a touch more water during cooking. Once cooked, remove from the heat and allow the stew to stand undisturbed for a few minutes before serving.

4 When ready to serve, heat a little oil in a frying pan and cook the chopped garlic until golden brown, not burnt. Scatter the garlic over the casserole and sprinkle with a little chopped fresh coriander. Serve with plain white rice and a dressed green salad.

250 g piece of streaky bacon, preferably smoked (use gammon steak if less fat is desired)

2 tablespoons olive oil, plus extra for frying the garlic

1 small onion, peeled and chopped

2 cloves garlic, peeled and crushed

1 carrot, diced

1 green chilli, deseeded and chopped

1 teaspoon ground coriander

250 g lentils

400 g canned peeled tomatoes

500 ml water

Pinch of salt

3 cloves garlic, peeled and chopped

Chopped fresh coriander to garnish

Serves 4–5

CHICKPEA SALAD WITH TUNA & ONIONS

Highly nutritious and tasty, this salad provides a good quantity of protein. It can be thrown together at the last minute if packaged precooked chickpeas and canned tuna are used.

1 Soak dried chickpeas overnight in plenty of cold water. Once soaked, place in a saucepan, cover with water and fast-boil for 10 minutes. Reduce the heat and simmer for 30 minutes, until tender. Drain and leave to cool. Alternatively, if using ready-to-use bottled or canned varieties, simply drain before use.

2 Place the cold, cooked chickpeas in a bowl and flake the fish over them. Then pour the vinaigrette over the contents of the bowl, season with salt and pepper and mix well.

3 To serve, slice the onion very thinly and spread over the chickpea and tuna mixture. Garnish with the chopped fresh parsley.

400 g cooked chickpeas (or canned or bottled varieties)

200 g fresh or canned tuna, grilled

Balsamic Vinaigrette (see opposite)

Salt and pepper to taste

1 large red onion, peeled

Large bunch chopped fresh parsley

Serves 4–5

3 Main Meals

FISH

POULTRY

BEEF

LAMB

PORK

Seafood Paella

The mix of fresh seafood, rice and vegetables has made paella hugely popular far beyond the borders of Spain. Its characteristic yellow colour is due to the powdered saffron. Meats such as chicken, pork, ham and chorizo (or spicy sausage) can also be added to make this into an even more robust and flavourful dish.

FOR THE STOCK

1 litre water

1 kg mussels (in their shells)

250 g uncooked prawns

1 carrot, 1 leek and 2 sticks celery, chopped

2 bay leaves

Handful of fresh parsley stalks

10 peppercorns

FOR THE RICE

4 tablespoons olive oil

1 onion, peeled and cut into rings

2 cloves garlic, peeled and chopped

1 small green pepper, deseeded and chopped

1 tomato, skinned and chopped

400 g short-grain rice

Pinch of saffron strands, dried and powdered (see page 19)

1 litre dry white wine

Salt and pepper to taste

250 g baby squid, cleaned

Lemon wedges to serve

Chopped fresh parsley to serve

Garlic Mayonnaise to serve (see page 90)

Serves 6

1 Bring the water to a boil in a large saucepan. Scrub the mussels under cold running water with a small, stiff brush, discarding any that are open or have damaged shells. Place in the boiling water until they begin to open, then lift them out and place in a colander to drain. Make sure the colander is sitting on a dish so you can collect the liquid that drains from the cooked mussels. This can be used when making the fish stock. Set the mussels aside and allow them to cool.

2 Plunge the prawns into the boiling mussel water, then remove them almost immediately so they do not overcook and toughen. Allow to cool. Peel the prawns, retaining the heads and shells, then set aside with the mussels. To make the stock, place the heads and shells back into the water and add the chopped carrot, leek, celery, bay leaves, fresh parsley stalks and peppercorns. Do not add salt, as the mussels themselves will provide a sufficient quantity. Simmer for 30 minutes then strain, reserving the liquid.

3 Meanwhile, heat the olive oil in a shallow, flameproof earthenware dish or paella pan (approximately 30 cm in diameter) and gently fry the onion rings, garlic, pepper and tomato for approximately 5 minutes.

4 Add the rice and stir, making sure all the grains are well coated in oil. When the grains become slightly translucent, sprinkle on the dried and powdered saffron (see page 19) and add the dry white wine.

5 Pour the reserved fish stock on to the rice and stir. Check the seasoning, adding salt if necessary. Boil the mixture for 5 minutes, then reduce the heat and simmer uncovered for a further 15 minutes. From time to time, use a large spoon to manoeuvre the rice from the edges of the pan into the centre, then stir.

6 About 5 minutes before the rice is cooked, when most of the liquid has been absorbed, place the uncooked squid into the simmering rice and stir. Arrange the cooked mussels and prawns on the paella to heat. Add more water or wine if the dish becomes too dry.

7 Remove from the heat and allow the paella to rest for 5 minutes. The rice should be *al dente*, or firm to bite, but still moist. Do not worry if it sticks to the base of the pan a little.

8 Serve directly from the cooking dish, garnished with lemon wedges, chopped fresh parsley and Garlic Mayonnaise (see page 90).

FISH PILAF

500 g fish, smoked or salted

3 eggs

3 tablespoons olive oil

1 small onion, peeled and chopped

2 cloves garlic, peeled and chopped

1 teaspoon ground cumin

1 teaspoon ground coriander

1 bay leaf

2–3 pieces lemon rind (pared with a potato peeler)

300 g Basmati rice

Salt and black pepper to taste

Cayenne pepper to taste (optional)

600 ml water

Juice of 1 lemon

Chopped spring onions or snipped fresh chives to serve

Chopped fresh coriander to garnish

Serves 4

Similar to kedgeree, this pilaf can be made using any fish that has a strong flavour, such as haddock or cod. Alternatively, try salted fish which is often cod and is known as 'bacalao' in Spain and 'baccalà' in Italy. You can use brown rice in place of Basmati for a bulkier dish, but if you do, increase the cooking time to 30 minutes.

1   If you are using salted fish, soak it for 12–24 hours, changing the water every 4–5 hours. This process softens the flesh and reduces the level of salt in the fish with each change of water. Once you have drained the last batch of soaking water, pour some boiling water on to the fish, then cover and allow it to soak for roughly 15 minutes to allow the flesh to soften.

2   Place the eggs in a small pan of boiling water, return to a boil, then simmer gently for approximately 10 minutes. Remove the cooked eggs from the heat and drain, then plunge them into cold water. Allow to stand for a few minutes, then remove the shells and set aside the hard-boiled eggs.

3   Heat the olive oil over medium heat in a large frying pan that has a lid. Fry the onion and garlic for 5 minutes, then add the cumin, coriander, bay leaf and lemon rind. Stir well to ensure that all the ingredients are thoroughly mixed.

4   Wash the fish and remove the skin. Cut the fish into 2–3 cm-long chunks and add these to the pan. Mix all the ingredients together well and continue to cook for 1 more minute.

5   Wash the rice thoroughly and drain, then tip it into the pan with the fish, stirring continuously to ensure that all the grains are properly coated in oil and spices. Season the mixture generously with salt and pepper and add as much cayenne pepper as you wish, according to how spicy you would like to make the pilaf.

6   Pour in the water and bring slowly to a boil. Mix everything thoroughly, then reduce the heat and simmer covered for exactly 10 minutes. Stir the pilaf once or twice during cooking to make sure it does not stick to the base of the pan.

7   Once the pilaf has cooked for 10 minutes, remove from the heat, take off the lid and squeeze a little lemon juice over the mixture. Give it one last stir, then remove the bay leaf and lemon rind and discard. Allow the pilaf to stand in the pan for 2–3 minutes before serving.

8   Spoon the pilaf into a serving dish. Cut the hard-boiled eggs into wedges and arrange them attractively around the rice. Finally, sprinkle chopped spring onions or chives and chopped coriander over the pilaf to serve.

SWORDFISH IN
CAPER & TOMATO SAUCE

*Swordfish has a wonderful meaty texture and its firmness makes
it ideal for baking, grilling or poaching. To depart from the usual
swordfish steaks, the recipe here offers an easy approach to preparing
this fish. The strident flavours of the tomatoes and capers complement
the milder taste of the fish. Serve this dish either hot or cold.*

800 ml Tomato Sauce (see below)

1 kg swordfish, in one piece
with skin left on

2 tablespoons capers

Handful of chopped fresh parsley
to garnish

Serves 6

1   First prepare the Tomato Sauce (see below), then place the whole piece
    of fish, skin-side down, into the simmering sauce, cover and cook gently
    for 40 minutes. Carefully turn the fish over halfway through cooking.
    (It is advisable to use a fairly small, deep saucepan so that the sauce
    covers most of the fish.)

2   Check the swordfish – if it is ready, the flesh in the middle of the fish will
    be opaque and the whole of the flesh will be cooked through but not dry.

3   Add the capers and leave to rest for 5–10 minutes before serving. Slice
    the swordfish thickly and serve with plenty of Tomato Sauce and a
    generous sprinkling of chopped fresh parsley. This dish is very good
    with a serving of Mashed Potatoes with Olive Oil (see page 72) and
    a green vegetable.

TOMATO SAUCE

This recipe produces a delicious basic tomato sauce that can be served either
hot or cold with a large variety of dishes. The quantities given here make
800 ml, which serves approximately 6.

Heat 1 tablespoon of oil in a large saucepan over medium heat, then add
1 small onion, peeled and chopped. Soften the onion for a couple of minutes,
then add 1 kg of chopped very ripe tomatoes, 2 peeled and crushed cloves of
garlic, 2 bay leaves, 2 chopped sticks of celery, 1 teaspoon of sugar and some
salt and freshly ground black pepper. Bring slowly to a boil and stew gently
for roughly 30 minutes until all the ingredients are well-cooked and pulpy.
Remove the bay leaves, then place the stewed tomato mixture in a food
processor and blend or pass through a sieve to remove the pips and skin.
Alternatively, if you do not have a food processor, pass the mixture through
a mouli. To serve hot, reheat the sauce very gently.

COLD SWORDFISH IN TOMATO CREAM

Once the poached swordfish is cooked, allow it to cool, then slice it thinly.
Place the cold tomato sauce in which the fish was cooked into a food processor
and add 150 ml of mayonnaise and 4 anchovy fillets. Process the mixture into
a smooth cream. If you are working without a blender, pound the anchovies in
a mortar with a pestle until finely crushed and whisk into the mayonnaise
before adding the capers. Pour the sauce over the sliced fish, sprinkle with
chopped fresh parsley and serve.

POACHED CHICKEN & VEGETABLES WITH RED & GREEN SAUCES

1 chicken, medium-sized

Vegetables for stock: 2 carrots, 1 onion, peeled, and 2 sticks celery, all chopped

2 bay leaves

Handful of fresh parsley stalks

Salt to taste

6 peppercorns

4 potatoes, medium-sized, peeled and chopped

4 carrots, medium-sized, chopped

4 leeks, chopped

4 small courgettes

Serves 4

Simple, healthy poached chicken with vegetables can be transformed into something a little bit special with colourful red and green sauces (see right).

1   Place the whole chicken in a large pan that has a lid. Add the chopped stock vegetables, bay leaves, parsley stalks, salt and peppercorns. Cover with water and bring slowly to a boil. Once the water is boiling, reduce the heat and simmer covered for approximately 1 hour or until the chicken is very tender.

2   Meanwhile, place the prepared potatoes, carrots and leeks in a large saucepan of boiling water. Cook for approximately 10 minutes until the vegetables are just softening, then add the courgettes and cook for a further 5 minutes until all the vegetables are cooked through and fairly soft.

3   Once everything is cooked, joint the chicken and place it on a large, heated serving dish. Arrange the cooked vegetables around the chicken pieces. Serve with *Salsa Verde* and *Salsa Rossa* (see below). The stock made from the chicken can be reserved and used for other recipes, such as soups and risottos. Store it in a sealed container and keep in the refrigerator for 3 days or freeze for up to 3 months.

SALSA VERDE (GREEN SAUCE)

This is a sharp sauce made from capers and anchovies, which is ideal as an accompaniment to poached chicken or fish and meat dishes. The recipe given here serves 4–6.

Place 350 g of chopped fresh parsley, 1 small can of anchovies, 2 peeled and crushed cloves of garlic, 3 tablespoons of capers, 1 small onion, peeled and chopped and 4 tablespoons of white wine vinegar in a food processor and blend, or purée by hand in a mortar using a pestle. Trickle in 100 ml of olive oil slowly and continue blending into a smooth but thickish sauce. If the sauce becomes too thick, add a little water.

SALSA ROSSA (RED SAUCE)

This piquant and colourful spicy sauce made from red peppers and tomatoes can be used hot or cold to enhance any vegetable dish. This recipe serves 4–6.

Heat 2 tablespoons of olive oil in a saucepan and fry 1 medium-sized onion, peeled and chopped, and 1 large red pepper, deseeded and chopped. Cook gently until soft, but not brown, then add 4 chopped tomatoes and a pinch of both salt and chilli powder. Simmer covered for roughly 30 minutes until the vegetables are reduced to a pulp. Add a little water if necessary. Place the reduced pulp in a food processor and blend or pass through a sieve until the consistency is that of a runny purée.

CHICKEN BREASTS ROLLED WITH HAM & CHEESE

The ham and cheese rolled inside these flattened chicken breasts make an attractive spiral pattern when the chicken is sliced (see left). The dish can also be served cold and is delicious with a fresh green salad and a generous dollop of mayonnaise.

4 chicken breasts, skins removed

Salt and pepper to taste

4 slices of Serrano ham or Parma ham

4 'fingers' (4 x 1 x 1 cm) Gruyère cheese

2 tablespoons vegetable oil

1 tablespoon butter

1 small onion, peeled and chopped

150 ml dry white wine

1 tablespoon gluten-free Dijon mustard

1 tablespoon tomato purée

Serves 4

1 To prepare the chicken breasts, cut horizontally into each piece of meat three-quarters of the way, then open out the breasts.

2 Place each opened breast between two sheets of greaseproof paper and, using a rolling pin, carefully pound them into thin, flat slabs of meat (or escalopes) of fairly even thickness. Avoid making holes in the meat. Remove the top sheets of paper and season the meat with salt and pepper.

3 Place a slice of ham and a finger of Gruyère cheese on each escalope and carefully roll up each bundle into a neat curl. Tuck in the ends of the chicken and secure each roll with a piece of string to help it keep its shape.

4 Melt the butter and heat the oil in a heavy-based saucepan or frying pan which has a lid. Cook the rolls in the fat, turning occasionally to brown them all over, then add the chopped onions. Once the onions have become translucent and the chicken rolls are browned, remove from the pan and keep warm on a heated plate covered with foil.

5 Deglaze the pan with the white wine (loosen the fat and the browned sediment at the bottom). Stir in the mustard and tomato purée and mix well. Return the chicken rolls to the pan and simmer covered for roughly 20 minutes. The chicken is cooked when the melted cheese begins to run out of the rolls.

6 Remove the chicken rolls from the sauce. Untie and discard the string. Slice each roll into 4–5 pieces, on a chopping board using a sharp knife. Arrange the slices attractively on a serving dish or on individual plates and pour the sauce around them. (If the sauce has reduced too much, add a little more wine and bring slowly to a boil to rescue it.) Serve with Potato Gratin (see page 72) or mashed potatoes and a green vegetable. If serving the dish cold – without the sauce – accompany with a green salad and a some Mayonnaise (see page 90).

CHICKEN BREASTS ROLLED WITH GOAT'S CHEESE AND HERBS

Flattened chicken breasts can also be rolled with goat's cheese and a mixture of herbs. Prepare the chicken as above and mash 125 g of goat's cheese with a bunch each of fresh shredded basil, chopped parsley, some thyme and also the juice of half a lemon. Spread the mixture on the escalopes and cook as above.

CHICKEN BREASTS STUFFED WITH RICOTTA

Chicken breasts are cooked in a wine and mustard sauce, then given richness with a melt-in-the-mouth ricotta and Parmesan stuffing.

1 Prepare the chicken breasts as for Chicken Breasts Rolled with Ham and Cheese (see opposite). Lay the chicken escalopes out on a chopping board and season with salt and pepper.

2 To make the stuffing, place all the ingredients in a mixing bowl and blend thoroughly using a fork.

3 Spread the ricotta mixture generously on to the chicken escalopes and carefully roll them up. Tuck in the ends and secure each roll with a piece of string. (This does not have to be done beautifully as the string will be removed later.)

4 Heat the oil and butter in a saucepan over medium heat and cook the rolled chicken pieces gently, turning occasionally to prevent them from becoming too brown.

5 Add the chopped onions, wine and mustard after roughly 10 minutes, then simmer gently for a further 20 minutes, turning the rolls from time to time. Once cooked, remove the chicken rolls from the sauce and allow to cool for 1–2 minutes. Remove the string and carefully slice each roll into 4–5 thick pieces using a very sharp knife. Place on a heated serving dish.

6 Stir the sauce remaining in the pan, adding a little more wine if there is too little moisture, or heating to reduce the liquid if it is too runny. (There should be roughly half the original quantity of liquid remaining.) Pour the sauce on to the rolled chicken slices, sprinkle with chopped fresh thyme or parsley and serve with Potato Soufflé (see page 73) and a green salad, or with Pesto Rice (see below).

FOR THE CHICKEN BREASTS

4 chicken breasts, skinned

Salt and pepper to taste

1 tablespoon olive oil and a knob of butter

1 small onion, peeled and chopped

150 ml dry white wine

1 tablespoon gluten-free Dijon mustard

2 teaspoons chopped fresh thyme or parsley to garnish

FOR THE RICOTTA STUFFING

225 g ricotta cheese

2 tablespoons freshly grated Parmesan cheese

1 teaspoon dried thyme

1 egg, medium-sized

Salt and pepper to taste

Serves 4

PESTO RICE

This aromatic and colourful rice dish is a delicious accompaniment to fish or chicken dishes. Served cold, it makes an ideal salad. This recipe serves 6.

Place 400 g of short-grain risotto rice in a saucepan that has a lid and mix in 100 ml of Pesto (see page 91). Make sure the grains are well coated in the pesto. Pour in 750 ml of boiling vegetable or chicken stock, add a little salt and stir. Bring to a boil, then reduce the heat and simmer covered for roughly 20 minutes. The rice should be just cooked – *al dente* or firm to bite – and quite dry. Carefully mix in another 100 ml of pesto, 2 peeled and chopped shallots and the juice of 1 lemon. Adjust the seasoning and serve hot or cold with 25 g of freshly grated Parmesan cheese. Decorate the rice dish with a few shredded basil leaves.

SPICED BEEF CASSEROLE

This warming winter dish can spice up any cold evening! The beef is cooked gently on the stove for a few hours, which allows the flavours of the spices and beer to be absorbed fully by the meat to create a delicious casserole.

2 tablespoons olive oil

1 kg stewing beef

3 cloves garlic, peeled and chopped

1 onion, peeled and chopped

1 teaspoon allspice

6 cloves

Freshly grated nutmeg to taste

300 ml dark beer, such as Guinness or stout

250 g prunes, soaked and pitted

Salt and pepper to taste

2 teaspoons arrowroot

Serves 6–8

1   Heat the oil over high heat in a large heavy-based casserole that has a lid. Cut the stewing beef into even-sized cubes and brown them rapidly in the heated oil. Reduce the heat and add the garlic, onion, allspice, cloves and nutmeg. Cook the meat for a few minutes until all the flavours are thoroughly blended together.

2   Pour in the beer and 125 ml water and slowly bring the stew to a boil. Then reduce the heat and add the prunes. Season the mixture with salt and pepper to taste. Cover the casserole and simmer gently until the beef is very tender – this will take approximately 2–3 hours, depending on the quality of the beef used. Stir once or twice during cooking.

3   Once the meat has cooked, blend the arrowroot with 2 tablespoons of water and stir this into the casserole. Bring the mixture back to a boil to thicken the sauce a little. Adjust the seasoning to taste. Serve the beef casserole with either plain boiled rice or some mashed potatoes and a green vegetable.

BRAISED STEAK WITH MUSHROOMS

This popular casserole uses cheaper cuts of beef, such as chuck steak, which are tenderised in tasty juices during the slow cooking process.

2 tablespoons olive oil

150 g smoked bacon or uncooked ham, diced

500 g braising steak

8 shallots, peeled

200 g button mushrooms

300 ml red wine

1 tablespoon tomato purée

1 tablespoon gluten-free Dijon mustard

1 teaspoon dried thyme (or mixed herbs)

Salt and pepper to taste

Serves 4

1   Heat the oil over medium heat in a heavy-based casserole that has a lid. Fry the diced bacon (or ham) for 5 minutes, until crispy, then remove from the casserole and set aside. Then brown the steak in the oil and bacon fat. Ensure that the meat is brown on both sides, then remove and set aside. Place the peeled shallots and mushrooms in the casserole and brown them for approximately 5 minutes.

2   Pour the wine into the casserole and bring to a boil. Add the tomato purée and the mustard and stir them in well. Sprinkle the dried thyme (or mixed herbs) over the mixture and season with salt and pepper. Place the steak back into the pan along with the bacon (or ham). Bring back to a boil, then simmer covered for approximately 2 hours until the meat is very tender. Turn the meat once during cooking.

3   When ready to serve, remove the steak, cut into 4 portions and place in a warmed serving dish. Reduce the sauce if it is too watery, then pour it over the steaks. Serve with plain boiled potatoes or mashed potatoes.

Marinated Beef with Olives

For an exciting alternative to the traditional beef casserole, try this recipe in which the beef is marinated in a sherry, herb and garlic mixture, then cooked with ham and olives (see above). The success of this dish depends on the quality of the beef used. Sirloin steak is suitable, but fillet steak is ideal.

1. To prepare the marinade, mix together the olive oil, sherry, onion, garlic, herbs, salt and pepper in a large bowl.

2. Slice the beef into thin strips and place into the bowl with the marinade. Ensure each piece is well coated in the liquid. Cover and leave to marinate for at least 2 hours.

3. When ready to cook, heat the oil over high heat in a heavy-based pan and fry the ham for 1–2 minutes. Then, when the pan is very hot, remove the beef from the marinade and add to the pan. Fry for 3–4 minutes only so the beef is not overcooked and tough. Turn the beef and ham regularly during cooking to ensure that the strips are evenly cooked all over. Remove the pan from the heat.

4. Meanwhile, place the marinade in a small saucepan over high heat and boil it vigorously to reduce the liquid to half the original amount, then pour it into the pan containing the beef and ham. Add the olives and reheat quickly so as not to continue cooking the beef. Serve immediately, with plain boiled rice or potatoes.

FOR THE MARINADE

150 ml olive oil

4 tablespoons dry sherry

1 onion, peeled and chopped

2 cloves garlic, peeled and crushed

1 teaspoon chopped fresh thyme or oregano

Salt and pepper to taste

FOR THE BEEF

1 kg fillet of beef or sirloin

Olive oil for frying

4 slices Parma or Serrano ham, cut into strips

15–20 green or black olives

Serves 6–8

STUFFED PEPPERS

Oil for greasing

225 g cooked rice (leftover risotto is ideal) or 75 g uncooked rice

1 tablespoon olive oil

1 small onion, peeled and chopped

2 cloves garlic, peeled and crushed

225 g minced beef, lamb or pork

1 tomato, skinned and chopped

2 teaspoons chopped fresh parsley

1 teaspoon chopped fresh oregano or thyme

50 g pine nuts

Salt and pepper to taste

2 large red peppers

2 tablespoons freshly grated Parmesan cheese

Serves 4

Delicious and sweet red or green peppers are roasted with a tasty stuffing of rice, cooked mince, pine nuts and herbs. I particularly enjoy this dish when served with a fresh home-made tomato sauce.

1 Preheat the oven to 180°C, gas mark 4. Grease a medium-sized roasting tin with oil. If you have to cook the rice, place it in a saucepan with plenty of boiling water and cook for 12–15 minutes until *al dente*, or firm to bite. Drain and set aside.

2 Heat the oil in a frying pan and cook the onion and garlic over low heat. Add the minced meat and cook for a further 10 minutes until the meat is browned and cooked through. (Cooked leftover minced meat may be used in place of raw mince, but should be cooked for only 1–2 minutes.) Add the tomato and herbs and cook for a further 2–3 minutes.

3 Add the cooked rice and stir well to ensure it absorbs the cooking juices. Mix in the pine nuts and season with salt and pepper. Stir well to combine all the ingredients, remove from the heat and allow to cool slightly.

4 Cut the peppers in half horizontally and remove all the seeds and pith. Spoon the stuffing into the peppers, pressing it in well to ensure all the crevices are filled.

5 Place the filled pepper halves into the roasting tin, ensuring they do not topple over, and cover with foil. Bake in the oven for 30 minutes. Remove the foil, sprinkle with the grated Parmesan cheese and bake uncovered for a further 30 minutes until the cheese is bubbling.

6 Serve the stuffed peppers with *Salsa Rossa* or Red Sauce (see page 56) or with fresh Tomato Sauce (see page 55) and a green salad.

STUFFED AUBERGINES
Aubergines can be stuffed in the same way as peppers. Cut them in half horizontally and scoop out as much flesh as possible without damaging the skins. Chop up some of the flesh and mix it in with the stuffing mixture (see above). Fill the aubergine halves with the stuffing, pressing down firmly. Cook them as for the peppers above, sprinkling them with grated Parmesan cheese before the final 30 minutes of cooking.

STUFFED TOMATOES
Tomatoes, like the peppers and aubergines, can also be stuffed with the mince, herbs and pine nut mixture. However, these will need less cooking time. Cut the tops off fairly large, firm tomatoes. Scoop out the flesh and seeds and discard them (or use them when making a tomato sauce). Fill the empty shells with the stuffing mixture (see above), pressing it into the tomato shells firmly. Sprinkle with grated Parmesan cheese and bake uncovered for 30 minutes.

MEATBALLS IN TOMATO & MUSHROOM SAUCE

Herbs, spices and a mixture of meats are combined in this unique recipe for juicy meatballs. A spicy mushroom and sherry sauce finishes the ensemble beautifully. This dish is equally good when made with minced lamb, but it is important that you buy meats of the best quality and have them finely minced so that they bind well during cooking.

1   Mix the minced beef and pork with the bacon, garlic, parsley, cumin and thyme in a bowl. Add the lemon juice and beaten egg and season with salt and pepper. Mix the ingredients together with your hands to ensure they are well blended. If you would like to test the seasoning, fry some of the mixture in a little oil and taste. The meatballs should be quite spicy, but tailor them to suit your preferences.

2   Divide the meat mixture evenly and roll it into balls that are roughly the size of golf balls. Dampen your hands with a little water before rolling the mixture – this will prevent it from sticking to your hands.

3   Brown the meatballs in a heavy-based casserole with the oil. Do this in small batches, to ensure they are all evenly cooked. Once browned, transfer the meatballs to a dish and keep warm in a low oven.

4   To make the sauce, heat the oil in the same heavy-based casserole in which the meatballs were browned and soften the onion and garlic in the oil. Drain the mushrooms, reserving the soaking liquid, and chop them finely. Add them and the tomatoes to the pan. Cook for another minute or so.

5   Mix in the sherry, a little of the reserved mushroom soaking liquid, the bay leaf and the paprika. Slowly bring the sauce to a boil. Place the meatballs back into the casserole with the sauce, season with salt and pepper and cover. Simmer gently for 30 minutes, turning the meatballs occasionally to ensure that they cook evenly and do not dry out. Once cooked, sprinkle with chopped parsley and serve with boiled rice, mashed potatoes or Polenta (see page 46).

Ingredients

250 g finely minced beef

250 g finely minced pork

4 rashers streaky bacon, finely chopped

I clove garlic, peeled and crushed

I tablespoon chopped fresh parsley

I teaspoon ground cumin

I teaspoon dried thyme

Juice of I lemon

I egg, beaten

Salt and pepper to taste

I tablespoon olive oil

FOR THE SAUCE

I tablespoon olive oil

I onion, medium-sized, peeled and chopped

I clove garlic, peeled and crushed

20 g dried mushrooms, soaked

3 tomatoes, peeled and chopped, or 200 g canned tomatoes

150 ml dry sherry

I bay leaf

I tablespoon paprika

Salt and pepper to taste

Chopped fresh parsley to garnish

Serves 4–5

MEAT LOAF

The same ingredients used for the meatballs (see above) can be combined to make a meat loaf. Include 100 g of cooked rice to lighten the texture a little. Instead of forming the meat mixture into balls, line a small loaf tin with rashers of streaky bacon and scoop the mixture into the tin, folding any excess bacon over the meat to surround it. Bake in the oven at 190°C, gas mark 5 for about 1 hour until the meat is cooked. Drain the meat juices from the mould into a jug to use as gravy. Carefully turn out the loaf and slice. Serve hot with the gravy and a green vegetable dish. Meat loaf is also excellent cold, on its own with a salad or in sandwiches.

Moroccan Lamb

*The spicy lamb is steamed in the oven for approximately 3 hours,
which makes it very tender and succulent (see right).*

2 cloves garlic, peeled

1 teaspoon coarse salt

2 tablespoons chopped fresh rosemary

1 tablespoon cumin seeds

1 tablespoon coriander seeds

2 tablespoons olive oil

2 tablespoons paprika

1 teaspoon cayenne pepper

1 leg of lamb (approximately
2 kg), boned

1 litre white wine

Serves 6

1 Crush the garlic and salt together in a mortar with a pestle, adding the
chopped rosemary, cumin seeds and coriander seeds gradually. Continue
grinding until all of the ingredients are broken down. Add the olive oil,
paprika and cayenne pepper and mix into a paste.

2 Place the leg of lamb, cut-side up, on a large sheet of tin foil and work half
of the spicy paste into it. Roll up the meat and secure with string. Rub the
remaining paste on to the outer surface of the roll and wrap in foil. Leave
for at least 3 hours, or overnight, to allow the spices to flavour the meat.

3 Preheat the oven to 180°C, gas mark 4. Unwrap the meat, leaving it tied,
and place in a roasting tin. Pour the wine around it and cover with another
sheet of foil. Seal the edges of the tin to prevent steam escaping.

4 Cook for 2 hours. Remove the foil, increase the heat to 200°C, gas mark 6
and cook for 1 more hour. If the pan juices dry out, add wine or water. To
serve, remove the string, cut the meat into thick slices and place on a bed
of Spicy Moroccan Rice (see page 68). Serve the pan juices as gravy.

Moussaka

*This popular Greek dish is usually drenched in a béchamel sauce (made
from wheat flour). This gluten-free version uses cornflour.*

3 aubergines, medium-sized

Salt for dehydrating

Olive oil for frying, plus extra for greasing

1 onion, peeled and chopped

2 cloves garlic, peeled and crushed

1 kg lamb, minced

1 tablespoon cornflour

1 teaspoon thyme or oregano

Salt and pepper to taste

3 large eggs

350 ml milk

400 ml fresh Tomato Sauce (see page 55)

Serves 4

1 Cut the aubergines into 1 cm-thick slices. Sprinkle with salt and set aside
for 1 hour to draw out the juices. Preheat the oven to 180°C, gas mark 4.
Grease a deep rectangular 20 x 28 cm ovenproof dish. Heat the oil in a pan
over medium heat, rinse the aubergines and pat them dry, then fry them
for a few minutes until slightly browned. Remove and set aside.

2 Place the onion and garlic in the pan and fry until transparent. Add the
mince and cook for 5 minutes until slightly browned. Mix in the cornflour,
herbs, salt and pepper and cook a little longer, then remove from the heat.

3 In a separate saucepan, beat the eggs with the milk, stirring and heating
until thick, without allowing the mixture to boil. (Some people may like
to add 50 g grated cheese at this stage – I do not think it necessary.)

4 Arrange the ingredients in three layers in the ovenproof dish – first some
aubergines, then the lamb, then the remaining aubergines. Pour over the
tomato sauce and top with the egg and milk sauce. Place in the preheated
oven for 1 hour or until the top is golden brown. Serve with a simple salad.

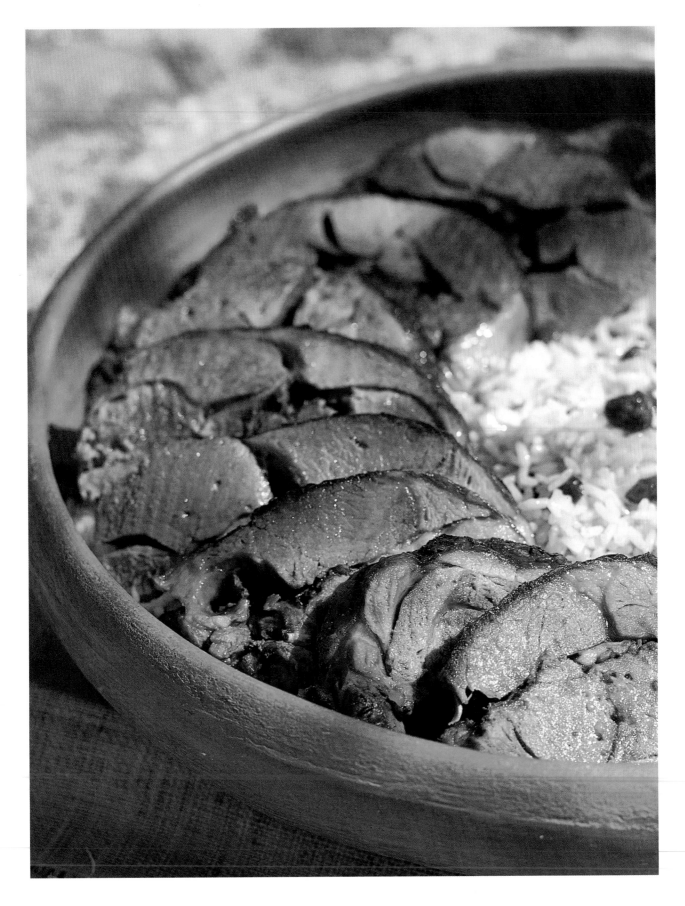

MARINATED & GRILLED
LAMB KEBABS

Cut a 700 g neck fillet of lamb into
2.5 cm cubes. Make a marinade by
mixing 4 tablespoons of olive oil, the
juice of 1 lemon, 4 peeled and
crushed cloves of garlic, 1 tablespoon
of chopped rosemary, 1 teaspoon of
cumin and salt and pepper. Marinate
the meat for about 1 hour. Remove
from the marinade and thread on to
skewers. Grill on a barbecue or in the
oven for about 10 minutes on each
side. You can also thread some
chopped red pepper, whole
mushrooms or chopped onion
on to the kebabs with the lamb.

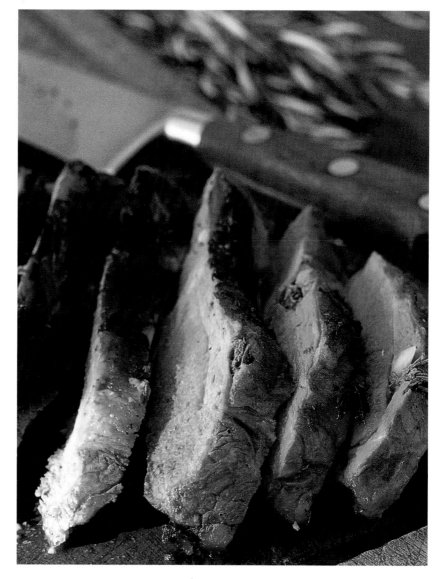

MARINATED & GRILLED LAMB

*Lamb is tenderised in a marinade of olive oil, lemon, rosemary and
garlic (see above). This dish is ideal for a special summer barbecue.*

I small leg or shoulder of lamb, boned
4 cloves garlic, peeled and sliced
I tablespoon dried rosemary
4 tablespoons olive oil
Juice of I lemon
I teaspoon ground cumin
Salt and pepper to taste
Serves 4

1 Butterfly the boned lamb (open it out) and pierce the flesh with a sharp
knife in several places. Push slivers of garlic and rosemary into the cuts.

2 Prepare the marinade in a large bowl by mixing together the olive oil,
lemon juice, ground cumin and salt and pepper. Place the meat into the
marinade and mix to ensure it is well covered. Leave for at least 1 hour.

3 Remove the lamb from the marinade and place either on an oiled barbecue
grill over hot coals or under a hot grill. Cook the meat for 15–20 minutes
on each side, brushing occasionally with the marinade.

BRAISED LAMB WITH AUBERGINE

The whole, boned leg of lamb is cooked in a casserole with aubergines, garlic and a mixture of spices. A thick sauce is made by blending the meat juices with the vegetables.

1 Slice the aubergines fairly thickly, sprinkle with salt and leave them to drain for at least 1 hour. This process will remove their bitter taste. Rinse and pat the slices dry.

2 Preheat the oven to 160°C, gas mark 3. Heat the oil in a large ovenproof casserole with a lid and cook the lamb for 5–10 minutes until brown all over. Remove from the dish and keep warm. (The joint does not need to be boned, but it does make the carving easier.)

3 In the same casserole, sweat (cook without browning) the chopped onion and garlic. Add the sliced aubergine and cook for a couple of minutes. Season with salt and pepper, sprinkle on the ground coriander and drop in the bay leaves.

4 Place the rolled lamb in the casserole – lay it on top of the aubergines and onion with the join facing down. Pour in the stock and lemon juice and stir in the tomato purée. Bring the mixture to a boil, then cover tightly with a lid or kitchen foil.

5 Place the casserole in the oven for 2 hours until the meat is very tender and the vegetables are very soft. Remove the tin foil covering, increase the oven temperature to 200°C, gas mark 6, and cook for a further 15 minutes or so. This will brown the meat and improve its appearance.

6 Transfer the joint to a serving dish and allow to rest in a warm place for 5–10 minutes, then remove the string. Meanwhile, put the vegetables and cooking juices into a bowl and mix with a hand-held blender to produce a thick sauce. Alternatively, pass the ingredients through a sieve. Place into a saucepan and reheat.

7 When the lamb is ready to serve, carve the meat into thick slices. Sprinkle with chopped fresh coriander and serve the sauce separately. This lamb dish is very good served with Fennel with Beans (see page 82) or some plain boiled rice.

2 aubergines, medium-sized

3 tablespoons olive oil

1 leg of lamb, boned and rolled

1 large onion, peeled and sliced

4 cloves garlic, peeled and chopped

Salt and pepper to taste

1 teaspoon ground coriander

2 bay leaves

500 ml chicken or beef stock

Juice of 1 lemon

1 tablespoon tomato purée

Chopped fresh coriander to garnish

Serves 4–5

BRAISED LAMB CHOPS

Lamb chops can be braised in a similar way to the leg of lamb described in the recipe above. For 4 servings, use 8 lamb chops. Brown them on both sides and lay them on the aubergines. Follow the recipe above, but cook the lamb chops in the oven for a shorter time – approximately 1 hour – in only 300 ml of stock. This results in vegetables that are not as cooked as in the recipe above, so serve them whole, rather than puréed into a sauce.

PORK FILLET WITH APRICOTS

2 tablespoons olive oil

Knob of butter

700 g pork fillet (tenderloin)

4 shallots, peeled and chopped

225 g ready-to-eat dried apricots

1 bay leaf

1 teaspoon cinnamon

Salt and pepper to taste

300 ml Port or Malaga wine

300 ml beef stock

1 tablespoon gluten-free Dijon mustard

Serves 4

A unique sauce, flavoured with apricots and sweet wine, is the secret of this dish, which is quick and easy to make.

1   Heat the oil and butter in a frying pan that has a lid. Add the pork fillet and cook until brown all over. Remove, cut into 4 pieces and keep warm.

2   Add the shallots and fry for 5 minutes, then put in the apricots, bay leaf, cinnamon, salt, pepper, wine and stock. Bring to a boil, then simmer for 10 minutes, stirring occasionally, until the liquid has reduced to half the original quantity. Mix in the mustard.

3   Place the pork fillets back in the pan and cook covered for 15 minutes, turning once. Remove the fillets, place on to 4 plates, pour the sauce over each helping and serve with Spicy Moroccan Rice (see below).

SPICY MOROCCAN RICE

Wash 200 g of Basmati rice and place it in 400 ml of salted water. Bring to a boil and simmer for 10 minutes. Mix in 2 peeled and chopped shallots, 50 g of seedless raisins, half a teaspoon each of ground coriander and ground cumin, a pinch of cayenne pepper, 1 tablespoon of olive oil and the juice of half a lemon. Leave to stand covered for 5 minutes to allow the flavours to permeate the rice.

PORK LOIN STUFFED WITH PATE

FOR THE PATE

200 g pig's liver, minced

200 g belly of pork, minced

100 g smoked bacon or ham, finely chopped

1 clove garlic, peeled and crushed

1 small onion, peeled and finely chopped

1 teaspoon dried thyme

1 tablespoon brandy

Pinch of allspice

Salt and pepper to taste

Butter for greasing

When this dish is served, the centre of each slice of pork is filled with a neat circle of delicious pâté (see right) – an impressive detail that is ideal for special dinner parties. The trick is to freeze the pâté in a sausage shape, in order to stuff the pork loin with ease.

1   To make the pâté, blend the minced meats together. Add the rest of the pâté ingredients and mix well. Leave to stand for roughly 1 hour to allow the flavours to infuse. To check the seasoning, fry a small amount of the mixture until cooked through, then allow to cool a little before tasting – it should be quite spicy. Adjust the seasoning if necessary.

2   Grease a sheet of foil that is roughly 30 cm long. Place the pâté mixture on to the foil and shape into a long sausage that is almost 30 cm long and roughly 4 cm in diameter. Wet your hands with a little water first, to prevent the pâté from sticking to them. Once you have formed the general shape, roll the sausage using the foil. Place in the freezer until solid.

3   The pork loin should be stuffed with the frozen roll of pâté about 24 hours before it is cooked. To do this, make a cross-shaped incision through the centre of the meat using a long, sharp knife. Cut into the loin from both

sides, then push the frozen pâté roll through the joint to the other side, coaxing it gently where necessary. Mould the meat around the pâté roll to ensure that the pâté maintains its circular shape. Season the stuffed loin with salt and pepper and, if using fatless loin, wrap it in rashers of streaky bacon. Wrap the joint in foil and set aside until the pâté has defrosted.

4   When ready to cook, preheat the oven to 180°C, gas mark 4. Place the stuffed pork loin, wrapped in bacon and covered with foil, in a baking tin with a little water around it. Bake in the preheated oven for roughly 2 hours. After this, remove the foil and increase the heat to 190°C, gas mark 5. Roast the pork for approximately 1 more hour, until the pork joint is brown.

5   Take the joint out of the baking tin and keep warm on a dish covered with aluminium foil. Now make a gravy by deglazing the baking tin with the stock and mustard. Then boil vigorously for 1–2 minutes to reduce the liquid a little.

6   When ready to serve, cut the meat into fairly thick slices and pour some gravy over each portion. Serve with roast or boiled new potatoes and a vegetable purée.

FOR THE PORK LOIN & GRAVY

1 kg pork loin, rindless

8 rashers streaky bacon (if using fatless pork loin)

250 ml stock

1 tablespoon gluten-free Dijon mustard

Serves 6

4 Vegetable & Side Dishes

POTATOES

MUSHROOMS

PEPPERS

VEGETABLE GRATINS

BEANS

MIXED VEGETABLES

TOMATOES

SALADS

SAUCES

POTATO GRATIN

100 g butter, melted
900 g potatoes, peeled
Salt and pepper to taste
Freshly grated nutmeg to taste
500 ml milk
Serves 6

This mouthwatering dish is an ideal accompaniment to any grilled meat or fish.

1 Preheat the oven to 190°C, gas mark 5. Brush a 20 x 30 cm gratin dish with a little of the melted butter.

2 Finely slice the peeled potatoes, using a mandolin, if possible. Arrange the sliced potatoes in layers in the gratin dish – brush each layer with melted butter, then season with salt, pepper and a little freshly grated nutmeg before arranging the next layer on top. Continue in this way until the potato slices are all used, ensuring you do not fill the dish right up to the top, so that the milk does not boil over during cooking.

3 Before you brush the last potato layer with melted butter, pour the milk into the dish up to a level just below the top layer of potatoes. Brush on the remaining melted butter and season with salt, pepper and grated nutmeg.

4 Cover the gratin with foil and place in the preheated oven for 45 minutes. Remove the foil and return to the oven for another 45 minutes, until the top of the gratin is brown and crispy and the potatoes are cooked through.

POTATO GRATIN VARIATIONS

If you would prefer this dish to be less rich, substitute vegetable or chicken stock for the milk. To make the dish more creamy, replace some of the milk with single or double cream.

Include thinly peeled and sliced onions or freshly grated cheese between the potato layers for additional flavour, or top the entire dish with freshly grated Parmesan cheese.

Another variation for potato gratin is to flavour the melted butter with garlic and mixed dried herbs – simply crush a clove of garlic into the butter and sprinkle with some herbs.

MASHED POTATOES WITH OLIVE OIL

1 kg potatoes, peeled and cut
200 ml hot milk
4 tablespoons extra virgin olive oil
Salt and pepper to taste
Serves 6

Substituting olive oil for butter produces a highly flavoursome mashed potato that is ideal for serving with casseroles and grilled meat.

Boil the peeled and cut potatoes in a large saucepan for 10–15 minutes, until soft. Drain thoroughly, then return them to the pan. Mash the potatoes while pouring in the hot milk a little at a time, until all the milk is used up and the mashed potato is creamy; more hot milk can be added if necessary. Add the oil and season with salt and pepper.

POTATO SOUFFLE

The addition of mashed potato to a basic soufflé results in a tasty and substantial side dish that is great served with grilled fish.

| 1 kg potatoes |
| 5 eggs, medium-sized, separated |
| 100 g butter, plus extra for greasing |
| 125 ml single cream |
| Salt and pepper to taste |
| Freshly grated nutmeg to taste |
| Serves 6 |

1   Preheat the oven to 180°C, gas mark 4. Lightly grease a 1.5 litre soufflé dish with melted butter.

2   Peel and chop the potatoes and boil for 10–15 minutes, until soft. Drain thoroughly, then mash until creamy.

3   Add the egg yolks, butter, cream, salt and pepper and a little grated nutmeg over the dish. Mix the ingredients together thoroughly.

4   Beat the egg whites until stiff and fairly dry and then fold into the potatoes. Pour the potato mixture into the greased soufflé dish and bake in the preheated oven for 45 minutes until the centre is set. Shake the dish gently – if the centre wobbles just slightly, it is set; if it wobbles dramatically, return the soufflé to the oven for a little longer.

SPICY POTATOES IN TOMATO SAUCE

In this side dish, chunky potato wedges are cooked in a fresh tomato sauce that is flavoured with a delicious blend of herbs and spices. Make the sauce as mild or as fiery as suits your own taste. Serve the dish with grilled meats.

| 600 g potatoes |
| Oil for frying |
| 1 clove garlic, peeled and chopped |
| 1 tablespoon wine vinegar |
| 1 tablespoon paprika |
| 1 teaspoon ground cumin |
| 1 teaspoon dried oregano |
| Pinch of chilli powder (or to taste) |
| 300 ml fresh Tomato Sauce (see page 55), or canned or bottled |
| Chopped fresh parsley to garnish |
| Serves 4–6 |

1   Peel the potatoes and cut them into 2 cm cubes. Heat the oil in a heavy-based pan and sauté the potatoes for 10–15 minutes until cooked through and brown on the outside.

2   Add the chopped garlic, vinegar, paprika, ground cumin, oregano and chilli powder and cook for a minute or two, stirring well to blend all the flavours thoroughly.

3   Add the tomato sauce – fresh sauce is ideal (see page 55), but any of the canned or bottled varieties may also be used. Heat the dish through until the sauce is bubbling nicely. Serve with a generous sprinkling of chopped fresh parsley.

SPICY SWEET POTATOES

An interesting variation on this recipe is to use sweet potatoes instead of the ordinary ones. The sweetness contrasts well with the spicy tomato sauce. Pesto (see page 90) is also delicious with sautéed potatoes of any kind.

ROSTI

*Made without any added fat, flour or eggs to bind it (see inset, right),
this potato cake is excellent to serve with roasted or grilled meat.*

600 g potatoes

Knob of butter

1 tablespoon olive oil

Salt and pepper to taste

Serves 4

1   Parboil the potatoes in their skins for 10 minutes. Drain and set aside to cool. Peel the potatoes and grate them using a coarse grater – this is easier to do if they are chilled beforehand.

2   Heat the butter and oil in a 20 cm non-stick frying pan. Spread the grated potatoes evenly in the pan, patting them down firmly. Reduce the heat to a low setting, season with salt and pepper and cook for 10 minutes.

3   Turn the rösti over to brown the other side. To do this, place a plate over the pan and turn the potato cake out on to it, then quickly slide it back into the pan. (Add a touch more oil at this point if the pan looks dry.) Cook the second side for 10 minutes then divide the rösti into 4 equal portions and serve. You may find that the rösti refuses to hold together, but this does not matter as it will be delicious anyhow.

VARIATIONS ON ROSTI

Individual rösti can also be made by forming a few small patties rather than one large one with the grated potatoes. Mould them in the palm of your hand, pressing the potato mixture together firmly, then fry them in plenty of oil for roughly 5 minutes on each side.

Flavourings can be added to the grated potato mixture, but do bear in mind that these should be fairly strong flavours in small quantities, as there is nothing except the natural potato starch to act as a binder. Adding a few chopped anchovy fillets to the grated potato makes a delicious fish cake. Some grated onion or fresh parmesan cheese also makes an interesting addition and any herb will give the rösti an aromatic flavour.

ROAST POTATOES WITH ROSEMARY & GARLIC

600 g potatoes

4 tablespoons olive oil

Salt and black pepper to taste

2 tablespoons rosemary leaves, chopped

2 cloves garlic, peeled and chopped

Serves 4–6

1   Preheat the oven to 220°C, gas mark 7. Peel the potatoes and cut them into 2 cm cubes. Parboil them in salted water for 5 minutes, then drain.

2   Pour the oil into a large roasting tray and heat it on the stove. Add the potatoes, turning them to ensure they are well coated in oil. Season with salt and plenty of freshly ground black pepper. Sprinkle chopped rosemary and garlic over the potatoes and place the tray in the top half of the oven for 30 minutes until they are brown and crispy all over (see right), turning them once or twice during cooking.

MUSHROOMS WITH LEMON & THYME

250 g oyster or button mushrooms

2 tablespoons extra virgin olive oil

2 cloves garlic, peeled and crushed

Several sprigs fresh thyme

Juice of 1 lemon

Salt and black pepper to taste

Serves 4

This delicious concoction of mushrooms sautéed with garlic, lemon juice and fresh thyme (see above) can be served either as a starter or as part of a main meal with grilled meat or fish.

1   Wash and trim the mushrooms and slice any that seem too large. Heat the oil in a shallow saucepan and, when hot, add the crushed garlic, the fresh thyme leaves (removed from their stalks) and the lemon juice. Cook for 2–4 minutes over medium heat.

2   Add the washed mushrooms to the pan and sauté gently for 15 minutes until cooked through. Season with salt and plenty of freshly ground black pepper. Remove from the pan and serve either hot or cold in individual terracotta dishes sprinkled with fresh thyme leaves.

MUSHROOMS WITH SERRANO HAM AND CHILLI

Heat 2 tablespoons of olive oil and 30 g of butter in a frying pan. Then add 6 chopped shallots and 1 crushed clove of garlic and cook for 5 minutes. Mix in 250 g of button mushrooms and cook for a further 3 minutes. Stir in 30 g of chopped Serrano ham, half a teaspoon of chilli powder, 4 tablespoons of water and 1 teaspoon of lemon juice and cook over high heat until the liquid has almost evaporated. Add 90 ml of red wine and cook until the liquid is reduced. Stir in another crushed clove of garlic and sprinkle with chopped fresh parsley.

MUSHROOMS STUFFED WITH PARMESAN CHEESE

These baked mushrooms, stuffed with garlic, herbs and cheese make an attractive starter or side dish.

1 Preheat the oven to 190°C, gas mark 5. Wash or brush the mushrooms, then remove the stalks. Set aside the caps and chop the stalks finely.

2 Mix the chopped stalks, garlic, parsley and Parmesan cheese with the olive oil. Add freshly ground black pepper, but not salt as the cheese is salty.

3 Brush the mushroom caps with olive oil and sit them in a baking tin or on a roasting tin. Divide the stuffing and spoon it into the mushroom caps. Cook in the preheated oven for 20 minutes. Remove from the oven, sprinkle with more fresh parsley, and allow to cool a little to serve.

4 large, flat mushrooms

2 cloves garlic, peeled and crushed

Handful of chopped fresh parsley

25 g freshly grated Parmesan cheese

2 tablespoons olive oil, plus extra for brushing

Freshly ground black pepper to taste

Serves 4

VEGETABLE-STUFFED MUSHROOMS
Make a vegetable purée using 100 g of a vegetable of your choice. Finely chop 2 shallots and fry until translucent. Remove from the heat and mix with the purée. Add ground coriander and salt and pepper to taste. Spread a tablespoon of purée on to each mushroom cap (prepared as above). Cook as above. Sprinkle with chopped fresh coriander to serve.

BLACK-EYE BEANS WITH MUSHROOMS

The smoky flavour of black-eye beans contrasts wonderfully with the earthy taste of mushrooms in this delicious side dish.

1 It is not necessary to soak black-eye beans before cooking. Boil the beans for 45 minutes, until tender. If desired, add a couple of bay leaves and a chopped onion to the water for extra flavour, but do not add salt. Once cooked, drain the beans and discard the bay leaves and onion.

2 Meanwhile, wash and trim the mushrooms and cut them into small pieces, if large. Heat the oil in a frying pan and add the mushrooms and garlic. Cook for 5 minutes, then add the lemon juice.

3 Remove the pan from the heat, add the cooked beans and mix well. Season the mushroom and bean mixture liberally with salt and plenty of freshly ground black pepper. Drizzle with a little olive oil and sprinkle with chopped fresh coriander to serve. This dish is also delicious mixed with rice – use 250 g cooked rice.

250 g black-eye beans

2 bay leaves (optional)

1 onion, peeled and chopped (optional)

250 g mushrooms (chestnut are good but any variety will do)

2 tablespoons olive oil

2 cloves garlic, peeled and crushed

Juice of 1 lemon

Salt and black pepper to taste

Chopped fresh coriander to garnish

Serves 4–6

Roasted Vegetables

1 red and 1 yellow pepper

1 large aubergine

2 small courgettes

Salt for dehydrating

1 bulb fennel

1 large onion, peeled

2 firm tomatoes

2 cloves garlic, peeled and crushed

4 tablespoons olive oil

Salt and black pepper to taste

Shredded fresh basil to garnish

Serves 4–6

Roasting vegetables with garlic and olive oil gives them a delicious flavour and brings out the sweetness of red and yellow peppers – try them as a meal or a side dish to serve with roasts and grills.

1 Chop the peppers into 2–3 cm squares. Cut the aubergine and courgettes into 2–3 cm cubes. Toss the aubergine in salt. Allow to stand for an hour or so to draw out the bitter juices, then rinse the cubes and pat them dry with kitchen paper.

2 Preheat the oven to 240°C, gas mark 9. Rinse the fennel and trim the root end. Cut off the stalks and feathery leaves, remove any bruised outer stalks, then slice the root into 2–3 cm cubes. Chop the onion and quarter the tomatoes.

3 Arrange all the vegetables on a shallow roasting tin and sprinkle with the crushed garlic. Toss all the vegetables in the oil, making sure they are all well coated and season liberally with salt and pepper.

4 Place the roasting tin in the top part the oven and roast for 30 minutes. Turn all the vegetables once during cooking. When done, they should be toasted and brown on the edges, but not overcooked. Serve either hot or cold with plenty of shredded basil leaves to decorate.

ROASTED AUBERGINE AND SWEET POTATO WITH SPINACH

Place 1 chopped aubergine in a bowl and stir in 2 tablespoons of olive oil. Add a pinch of cayenne pepper, a sprinkling of black pepper and half a tablespoon of lemon juice. Pour the mixture into a roasting tin with 1 chopped red pepper. Place 1 chopped sweet potato and 1 can of chickpeas in the bowl and add half a tablespoon of olive oil, half a tablespoon of lemon juice, a pinch of paprika and a little freshly grated nutmeg. Stir to blend, then place on the roasting tin.

Cook the vegetables in the oven at 240°C, gas mark 9 for 30 minutes, then mix in 55 g uncooked shredded spinach. Season with black pepper to taste. If the dish is too dry, add more olive oil or lemon juice. Serve with yogurt mixed with chopped mint.

ROASTED FENNEL

Trim 3 large bulbs of fennel and cut each into 6 wedges. Place the fennel in a mixing bowl and toss with 1 tablespoon of olive oil and plenty of salt and freshly ground black pepper. Place on a roasting tray and cook in the oven at 240°C, gas mark 9 for 1 hour until browned at the edges and tender.

ROASTED CARROTS AND PARSNIPS

Chop 400 g of peeled carrots and 400 g of peeled parsnips into 3 cm pieces. Mix with 200 g of peeled shallots and toss the vegetables in 1 tablespoon of olive oil, a pinch of dried thyme, a little salt and some freshly ground black pepper. Roast in the oven at 240°C, gas mark 9 for 1 hour until tender.

ROASTED PEPPER SALAD

Roasted peppers are so tasty that very little additional flavouring is needed. This dish is a good light first course (see right) and can be used as an accompaniment to many dishes, such as grilled or roasted meat or fish. I suggest red or yellow peppers, as these are easier to peel and attractively coloured.

1   Preheat the oven to 240°C, gas mark 9. Brush the peppers with a little oil and place them in the top half of the oven. Cook for 20–30 minutes, turning the vegetables once, until the skins are blackened and blistered and the flesh is soft.

2   Remove the peppers from the oven and place them into a plastic bag. Seal the bag immediately and allow the peppers to stand for 15 minutes, to loosen the skins.

3   Carefully peel the peppers, cut off the stem and scrape out the seeds, taking care not to damage the flesh. Cut the flesh into strips, place in a serving dish and drizzle lightly with olive oil. Season with salt and freshly ground pepper to taste and sprinkle with some chopped fresh coriander. Serve immediately.

4 large red peppers or yellow peppers (or a mixture of both)

Olive oil for brushing

Salt and black pepper to taste

Chopped fresh coriander to garnish

Serves 4–6

FRIED PEPPERS

Small and slim green peppers are best for this recipe (see right), in which they are pan-fried whole in olive oil and salt.

Heat the oil in a large frying pan over medium heat and cook the peppers whole, including the stems, for about 15 minutes, turning them from time to time. Do not overcook them – they are done when they become a little floppy and brown in places. Sprinkle with plenty of freshly ground sea salt and serve either hot or cold with grilled meat or fish.

PEPPER, TOMATO AND ANCHOVY RELISH

This tasty relish is based on green peppers and makes an ideal accompaniment to grilled meats. Chop 4 deseeded green peppers into strips and cut these into roughly 1 cm pieces. Chop 1–2 chillies and peel and chop 2 cloves of garlic. Roughly chop 4 canned anchovy fillets and skin and chop 4 medium-sized tomatoes. Heat 4 tablespoons of olive oil in a saucepan over medium heat, then add the peppers, chillies, garlic and chopped anchovies. Cook for about 5 minutes, stirring constantly to ensure that none of the ingredients stick to the pan or burn. Add the peeled and chopped tomatoes and allow the mixture to stew for roughly 10 minutes until the tomatoes have reduced to a pulp. Add salt if necessary. Serve sprinkled with chopped fresh parsley.

4 tablespoons olive oil

12 slim green peppers

Freshly ground sea salt to taste

Serves 4–6

FENNEL WITH CHEESE SAUCE

2 bulbs fennel

Knob of butter

300 ml Cheese Sauce (see page 91)

Serves 4

This combination of sweet, scented fennel topped with a rich cheese sauce is delightful.

1   Rinse the fennel and trim the root end. Cut off the stalks and feathery leaves, remove any bruised outer stalks and cut the fennel into quarters. Place in a large saucepan with the butter and 2–3 tablespoons of water. Cover the pan tightly and cook over low heat for 20 minutes, turning once, until just tender – do not overcook them. Add a little more water to the pan if necessary.

2   Transfer the cooked fennel to a warm serving dish (terracotta dishes are ideal for gratins) and pour over the Cheese Sauce (see page 91). Place under a grill for 10 minutes, then sprinkle with fronds of fennel to serve.

LEEK OR CAULIFLOWER WITH CHEESE SAUCE

Use cheese sauce with leeks or cauliflower in the same way as with fennel. With leeks, cut off the roots and trim the tops. Cut each leek in half lengthways to within 4 cm of the root ends. Separate the leaves and wash them thoroughly under running cold water. Cook in a large saucepan with a small amount of water for 10 minutes, until soft. Finally, pour over the cheese sauce and serve.

Cauliflower can be cooked whole in a large covered saucepan with boiling water for 15–20 minutes until soft. Serve the cauliflower whole with the cheese sauce poured over the top.

COURGETTE & SESAME GRATIN

Sesame has a wonderful nutty flavour that, combined with melted cheese, enlivens the taste of courgettes in this warming side dish. Serve it with meat dishes.

500 g courgettes

1 tablespoon sesame oil

4 cloves garlic, peeled and chopped

Salt and black pepper to taste

100 g cheddar cheese, coarsely grated

1 tablespoon sesame seeds

Serves 4

1 Wash and trim the courgettes then cut them into 1 cm-thick slices. Heat the sesame oil in a frying pan over low heat, then add the chopped garlic and sliced courgettes. Sauté gently for 5–6 minutes, turning the courgettes occasionally to cook them on both sides. Make sure you do not overcook them – they should remain *al dente*, or firm to bite. Add salt and freshly ground black pepper.

2 Place the cooked courgettes in a flameproof dish. Cover them with the grated cheese and sprinkle with the sesame seeds.

3 Grill the courgettes and cheese under medium heat for 3–4 minutes until the cheese begins to melt and sizzle and the seeds are slightly toasted. Ensure you do not burn the topping.

AUBERGINE GRATIN

Baked aubergines and tomatoes are given a golden melted cheese topping. Make sure you use cheese that melts properly when heated. Goat's cheese is best, due to its fairly strong flavour, but Mozzarella, Fontina or a mild Cheddar are also good.

4 large aubergines

Salt for dehydrating

2 tablespoons olive oil, plus extra for greasing

2 large tomatoes, peeled and thickly sliced

Salt and pepper to taste

2 teaspoons dried oregano

300 g cheese, thinly sliced

Serves 4

1 Cut the aubergine into 1 cm–thick slices. Sprinkle with salt and leave for 1 hour to draw out the bitter juices. (This process also ensures that the aubergines absorb less oil when fried.) Rinse the slices and pat dry with a sheet of kitchen paper. Preheat the oven to 200°C, gas mark 6.

2 Heat the oil in a frying pan and add the aubergine, a few slices at a time. Fry them quickly, turning them over during cooking to ensure that they are cooked through.

3 Grease a shallow ovenproof dish thoroughly with a little oil and arrange the slices of fried aubergine in the base of the dish in alternate layers with the peeled and thickly sliced tomatoes. Sprinkle on salt, pepper and a little of the oregano between each layer. Continue to layer the vegetables until all the ingredients are used up or until the dish is full.

4 Cover the aubergines and tomatoes with a layer of cheese slices and place the dish in the preheated oven. Bake for 30 minutes until the cheese has melted and is bubbling and the aubergines and tomatoes are piping hot. Remove the Aubergine Gratin from the oven and serve immediately with a dressed green salad.

GREEN BEANS WITH GARLIC & ALMONDS

Green beans fried in garlic and olive oil are topped with toasted almonds in this tasty side dish.

500 g green beans

2 tablespoons olive oil

4 cloves garlic, peeled and sliced

Salt and freshly ground black pepper to taste

50 g almond slivers, toasted, to serve

Serves 4

1 Preheat the oven to 180°C, gas mark 4. Top and tail the beans (and string them, if necessary) and cut each bean into 2–3 pieces. Drop them into a saucepan of boiling, salted water and cook until slightly tender. This will take roughly 5 minutes, but the cooking time does depend on the type of bean used. Do not overcook them – they should not be soft, but should retain some bite. Once cooked, drain the beans and set aside.

2 Heat the oil in a saucepan and fry the sliced garlic over medium heat for a few minutes until the slices begin to brown. Remove from the heat and add the cooked beans, tossing them around the pan to ensure they are coated in oil and garlic. Season with salt and plenty of freshly ground black pepper.

3 Toast the almonds by placing them on a baking tray and cooking in the preheated oven for 8–10 minutes until lightly browned. Stir occasionally during cooking to ensure the nuts colour evenly. Once cooked, sprinkle the almonds over the beans to serve.

GREEN BEANS WITH HAZELNUTS
Replace the almonds in the recipe above with roasted hazelnuts that have been fried in butter for 3 minutes. Mix them with 1 teaspoon of grated lemon rind and a pinch of cayenne pepper.

FENNEL WITH BEANS

I suggest flageolet beans for this recipe, but haricot beans are just as suitable. The soft-textured beans and crisp fennel contrast well.

250 g flageolet beans

1 bulb fennel

2 tablespoons olive oil

1 clove garlic, crushed

½ teaspoon cumin seeds

Salt and pepper to taste

Juice of ½ lemon to serve

Serves 4

1 If using dried beans, soak them overnight, then cook them as described on page 87. Otherwise, use canned or bottled, ready-cooked beans. Rinse and trim the fennel bulb, cut it in half and slice thinly. Heat the oil in a frying pan which has a lid and cook with the garlic over low heat for 5 minutes.

2 Add the cooked beans and the cumin seeds. Season with salt and pepper and cook covered for a further 10 minutes, stirring occasionally.

3 When ready to serve, squeeze the lemon juice over the beans and fennel and decorate with fennel fronds if you have any. This dish is very good with pork or ham and perfect served with Braised Lamb and Aubergine (see page 67).

BROAD BEANS & HAM

This protein-packed side dish also makes a hearty first course. It looks attractively rustic served in individual terracotta dishes (see below).

1   Shell the beans and place them in a saucepan of salted boiling water. Cook for 5–10 minutes until tender. (The cooking time for broad beans depends entirely on their size – the larger they are, the longer they take.) Ensure you do not to overcook them. Drain and set aside. If using large beans, remove the skin from each bean once cooked.

2   Heat the oil in a saucepan and gently fry the spring onions for 1–2 minutes until they begin to soften.

3   Add the strips of ham to the pan with the spring onions and cook for 2–3 minutes, stirring constantly, then add the cooked beans. Season with freshly ground black pepper and a little salt if necessary (the ham may be fairly salty itself) and cook for a few more minutes, stirring constantly, until the beans and ham are cooked. When ready to serve, divide the beans into 4 terracotta dishes and sprinkle with chopped fresh parsley.

1 kg broad beans

2 tablespoons olive oil

3–4 spring onions, chopped

100 g Parma or Serrano ham, cut into strips

Salt and black pepper to taste

1 tablespoon chopped fresh parsley to garnish, optional

Serves 4

BROAD BEAN SALAD

Small and tender broad beans that have been skinned and cooked make a tasty and filling salad on their own. Simply toss them in Vinaigrette (see page 91) and serve on lettuce leaves.

CHICKPEAS WITH SPINACH

The nutty texture of chickpeas and the softness of spinach purée in this recipe (see above) is a remarkably successful combination. In Spain, the dish is served as tapas or as an appetiser. It is great with grilled fish.

500 g fresh spinach (250 g frozen spinach may be used)

4 tablespoons olive oil

4 cloves garlic, peeled and crushed

400 g cooked chickpeas

1 teaspoon ground cumin

1 teaspoon paprika

Juice of 1 lemon

Salt and pepper to taste

Serves 4–6

1   If using fresh spinach, wash thoroughly and place in a large saucepan with only the water that clings to the leaves. Cook over low heat until the leaves start to wilt. (Cook frozen spinach according to packet instructions.) Drain thoroughly, squeezing out excess water, then chop finely.

2   Heat the oil in an open saucepan and gently fry the garlic for a couple of minutes until golden brown.

3   Add the chickpeas to the pan with the garlic, then add the cumin, paprika, lemon juice, salt, pepper and spinach. Simmer over low heat for roughly 20–30 minutes, stirring occasionally, until the spinach is reduced to a pulp. Adjust the seasoning and serve immediately.

COOKING PULSES

Pulses are very important ingredients in a gluten-free diet – besides being excellent sources of fibre, their uses in cooking are countless. There is also a huge range of choice with dried beans, peas and lentils.

Most dried beans should be soaked overnight, then cooked in plenty of boiling water which can be flavoured with a clove-studded onion or a bay leaf or two. However, never flavour the water with salt – this toughens the skins, as does any acidity such as tomato sauce or lemon juice.

It is important to fast-boil beans for at least 10 minutes at the beginning of cooking to remove the toxins. Then simmer the beans until cooked. The time taken to cook beans varies according to variety. It is worth experimenting with precooked, canned or bottled beans, as they are readily available, save time and can be just as tasty.

VEGETABLE 'SPAGHETTI'

This pretty side dish is an attractive and tasty accompaniment to almost any meal and makes a great alternative to the usual rice or potatoes.

1 Cut the vegetables into thin strips (julienne). Heat the oil in a wok or a frying pan, add the garlic, carrots and turnips and stir-fry for 3–4 minutes. Add the remaining vegetables and fry for a further 3–4 minutes until the vegetables are *al dente*, or firm to bite. Season with salt and pepper.

2 Place in a serving dish, then sprinkle with grated Parmesan cheese and decorate with shredded basil leaves to serve.

500 g mixture of carrots, courgettes, peppers, turnips, leeks and garlic

2 tablespoons olive oil

Salt and pepper to taste

Freshly grated Parmesan cheese to serve

A few leaves shredded fresh basil to serve

Serves 4–6

CARROTS WITH CUMIN

The flavours of cumin and carrots are successfully combined in this side dish, which is good served with lamb or pork.

1 Place the carrots in a saucepan with the stock. Bring to a boil, then simmer covered for 5 minutes, stirring once or twice, until *al dente*, or firm to bite.

2 Remove from the heat and drain any remaining liquid. Pour in the olive oil, add the cumin seeds and mix well. Season with freshly ground black pepper and some salt, if necessary – the stock may be salty enough in itself.

500 g carrots, washed and sliced into julienne or discs

125 ml concentrated chicken stock (1 gluten-free stock cube or fresh stock)

1 tablespoon olive oil

50 g cumin seeds

Salt and pepper to taste

Serves 4–5

CARROTS WITH MANGO CHUTNEY

Another appetising way to serve carrots is to cook them in stock as above, then, instead of adding cumin and oil, add 2 tablespoons of mango chutney. This produces a sweet-and-sour flavour that is perfect for pork dishes.

TOMATO & ARTICHOKE SALAD

Tomatoes and artichokes are combined with a balsamic vinaigrette to make a refreshing summer salad that is ideal with grilled or barbecued fish.

1 kg baby globe artichokes (or canned artichoke hearts)

4 tomatoes, medium-sized, firm but ripe

Balsamic Vinaigrette (see page 48) to taste

Salt and pepper to taste

Handful of chopped fresh parsley to serve

Serves 4–6

1   If using fresh baby globe artichokes, remove 2–3 rows of the tough outer leaves of each artichoke, then trim the stalk and cut off the cone-shaped tip to remove the tough pointed ends. Bring a saucepan of salted water to a boil, add the artichokes and boil for 10 minutes until tender. Drain and allow them to cool, then cut each artichoke in half and place in a mixing bowl. (Canned artichoke hearts are precooked, so can be halved without any preparation.)

2   Cut the tomatoes into wedges and place in the bowl with the artichoke hearts. Prepare the Balsamic Vinaigrette (see page 48) and pour it into the bowl, tossing the salad to ensure that the tomatoes and artichokes are all well coated in the dressing. Season with salt and pepper. To serve, sprinkle with chopped fresh parsley.

TOMATOES STUFFED WITH HERB RICE

Aromatic herb rice makes a perfect stuffing for tomato shells. Make sure you select tomatoes that are firm, but ripe, so that the skins are tough enough to hold their shape, yet have good flavour. This side dish is also good as a starter.

4 tomatoes, medium-sized, firm but ripe

100 g cooked rice of any kind

2 tablespoons mixed fresh herbs (chives, basil, parsley, tarragon), chopped

1 shallot, peeled and chopped

1 tablespoon olive oil

1 egg, hard-boiled, chopped

Juice of 1 lemon

Salt and pepper to taste

Chopped fresh parsley to garnish

Serves 4

1   Cut the tops off the tomatoes and carefully scoop out the seeds and pulp using a spoon, leaving the tomato shell empty and intact.

2   Place the rice in a bowl and mix in the fresh herbs. Add the shallot, olive oil, hard-boiled egg, lemon, salt and pepper and stir until all the ingredients are blended. Season the insides of the tomato shells and fill with the stuffing. Garnish with chopped fresh parsley to serve.

TOMATOES STUFFED WITH TUNA

Prepare 4 medium-sized tomatoes as for Tomatoes Stuffed with Herb Rice, above. Mash a 200 g tuna fish with 2 tablespoons of mayonnaise, using a fork. Mix in 1 tablespoon of chopped gherkins, 1 tablespoon of chopped celery and 1 peeled and chopped shallot. Season with plenty of freshly ground black pepper and some salt, if the fish is not salty enough itself. Season the insides of the tomato shells also before stuffing them with the tuna mayonnaise. Decorate the stuffed tomatoes with a small sprig of fresh parsley. Allow 1 tomato per serving.

TOMATOES BAKED WITH PARMESAN CHEESE

This tasty cheese and tomato snack (see above) can be served either hot or cold and makes an excellent accompaniment to almost any dish, particularly soups.

1   Preheat the oven to 220°C, gas mark 7. Grease a medium-sized baking tin thoroughly with a little olive oil. Slice the tomatoes thickly using a sharp knife and lay them out on the greased baking tin.

2   Make a paste by mixing together the grated Parmesan cheese, olive oil and chopped parsley. Season the paste with freshly ground black pepper (salt is not necessary as the cheese is quite salty itself). Spread a little of the cheese paste on to each slice of tomato and place the dish in the top of the preheated oven. Bake for 15 minutes until the tomatoes are softened and the cheese topping is browned and bubbling.

2 tablespoons olive oil, plus extra for greasing

2 large tomatoes, firm but ripe

50 g freshly grated Parmesan cheese

1 tablespoon chopped fresh parsley

Black pepper to taste

Serves 4

LETTUCE HEARTS WITH ANCHOVY DRESSING

The fresh and clean taste of crispy lettuce hearts contrasts wonderfully with the potency of anchovies in this light salad (see right). The ingredients can be beautifully presented to make an eye-catching side dish for special occasions.

2 lettuce hearts (Little Gem)

125 ml olive oil

1 tablespoon white wine vinegar

1 tablespoon ready-made mayonnaise

12 anchovy fillets

Freshly ground black pepper to taste

2 tablespoons chopped fresh parsley

4 cloves garlic, peeled and chopped and fried in olive oil (optional)

Serves 4

1 Wash and trim the lettuce hearts and set aside. To prepare the dressing, place the oil, vinegar, mayonnaise, four of the anchovy fillets and some freshly ground black pepper in a food processor. Blend the ingredients, then add the chopped fresh parsley. If you do not have a food processor, chop the anchovies finely and place them, along with the other ingredients, in a jar that has a lid. Shake the jar vigorously until all the ingredients are thoroughly combined.

2 To serve, cut the lettuce hearts into quarters and place two quarters on each plate. Drizzle the dressing over the lettuce hearts. Add a sprinkling of chopped and fried garlic if desired – this gives the dish a wonderful richness. Drape one anchovy fillet attractively over each lettuce heart quarter to decorate.

CARROTS WITH RAISINS & PINE KERNELS

This sweet and creamy salad combines crunchy carrots and nuts with soft raisins and smooth mayonnaise.

500 g carrots

3 tablespoons ready-made mayonnaise

2 tablespoons olive oil

Juice of 1 lemon

50 g seedless raisins

50 g pine kernels

Salt and pepper to taste

Snipped fresh chives to garnish

Serves 4–6

1 Peel the carrots or scrape them clean, then grate them using the coarse blade on your grater. Place the grated carrot in a large mixing bowl and add the mayonnaise, olive oil and lemon juice. Mix well until all the ingredients are thoroughly blended.

2 Add the raisins and pine kernels and mix well, ensuring that all of the mixture is well combined with the dressing. Season with salt and pepper and sprinkle with snipped fresh chives to serve.

CARROTS WITH APPLE AND DATES

The honey, mint and dates in this salad give it a hint of the Middle East. Mix 1 tablespoon of lemon juice, 1 teaspoon of honey, a quarter of a teaspoon of fresh mint and a pinch of salt in a large bowl until well combined. Peel or scrape the carrots clean and add to the bowl with 2 peeled, cored and shredded Granny Smith apples, 50 g of pitted and chopped dates and 2 tablespoons of chopped fresh parsley. Toss well to mix, then serve.

MAYONNAISE

1 egg yolk

½ teaspoon salt

1 teaspoon gluten-free Dijon mustard

225 ml oil (light olive or vegetable oil)

Juice of 1 small lemon

Makes 225 ml

Make sure that all the ingredients are at room temperature before making the mayonnaise. Combine the egg yolk, salt and mustard in a bowl and whisk the mixture thoroughly. Add the oil – to begin with, add a drop at a time, then slowly increase the flow, whisking the mixture continuously until all the oil is fully incorporated. (Avoid using virgin olive oil – this has too strong a flavour for mayonnaise.) Add the lemon juice and more salt if necessary. If the mixture is too thick, add a little warm water to dilute it, mixing well. Mayonnaise can be made easily if using a food processor – place 1 egg yolk and 1 whole egg in the processor with the salt, mustard, lemon juice and half of the oil. Blend together and, with the machine still running, add the remaining oil in a steady stream. Adjust the seasoning to taste.

GREEN MAYONNAISE

Add watercress to the basic mayonnaise and process in a blender to break down the watercress thoroughly. Green mayonnaise is delicious on cold fish or with hard-boiled eggs.

GARLIC MAYONNAISE

Add 1 crushed clove of garlic – or more, to taste – to the basic mayonnaise. Mix thoroughly to combine the garlic evenly with the other ingredients. Garlic mayonnaise is excellent on fish or as a dip for large prawns.

TUNA FISH MAYONNAISE (TONNATO)

Pound 2 anchovy fillets with a 50 g can of tuna fish in a little of the fish oil, adding a few finely chopped capers if desired, for additional flavour. Blend this mixture gradually into the basic mayonnaise. Tuna fish mayonnaise is particularly suitable for cold meats.

PESTO

2 cloves garlic, peeled

50 g pine nuts

Salt to taste

Shredded fresh basil (large bunch)

150 g light olive oil

50 g freshly grated Parmesan cheese

Makes 200 ml

Pound the garlic, pine nuts and salt in a mortar using a pestle. Add the shredded basil leaves, a few at a time, and continue pounding until all the ingredients are fully ground down. Pour in the oil gradually and continue mixing. Finally, stir in the freshly grated Parmesan cheese. Alternatively, the ingredients may be blended together in a food processor. Pesto may be kept for a few days if necessary – seal it well and store in the refrigerator.

TOMATO PESTO

Pound 2 cloves of garlic with salt (to taste) and 10 sun-dried tomatoes in a mortar with a pestle. Add the shredded basil leaves, the olive oil and 1–2 chopped chillies to taste.

WHITE SAUCE

Make a paste by mixing a little of the milk into the cornflour in a pan. Stir in the remaining cold milk, ensuring there are no lumps, place the pan over medium heat and slowly bring to a boil, stirring. Reduce the heat to simmer for 2–3 minutes until the sauce is thickened. Add salt and pepper.

300 ml milk

25 g cornflour

Salt and pepper to taste

Makes 300 ml sauce

CHEESE SAUCE

Add 100 g of grated cheese and 1 tablespoon of gluten-free Dijon mustard to the basic white sauce, stirring over low heat until the cheese melts. Cheese sauce is good on many vegetable or chicken dishes.

PARSLEY SAUCE

Mix a handful of chopped fresh parsley into the white sauce directly before serving. This sauce is ideal with plain white fish such as cod.

LEMON SAUCE

Use a little less milk in the white sauce recipe and add the juice of 1 lemon as the mixture begins to thicken. This sauce is good on fish or vegetables.

CAPER SAUCE

Add 2 tablespoons of finely chopped capers to the prepared white sauce just before serving. Caper sauce is delicious with plain poached fish or chicken.

ONION SAUCE

Fry a chopped onion in a little butter until transparent, then mix this into the white sauce. Onion sauce is particularly good on vegetables such as cauliflower or courgettes.

VINAIGRETTE

Place all the ingredients in a jar which has a lid and shake vigorously. Alternatively, blend the ingredients together in a food processor. Use as required.

50 ml white wine vinegar

250 ml olive oil

1 tablespoon gluten-free Dijon mustard

Pinch of salt

Makes 300 ml

VINAIGRETTE VARIATIONS

Any type of vinegar can be used: balsamic vinegar gives a deliciously sweet taste; sherry vinegar is stronger; scented vinegars add an exotic touch.

Any oil, or combination of oils, can be used: sesame oil gives a distinctive toasted flavour – only a little is recommended; extra virgin olive oil creates a strong, biting flavour; vegetable oil gives a lighter taste.

Add a tablespoon of chopped fresh herbs to the basic vinaigrette for a delightful aromatic touch, or a tablespoon of mayonnaise to create a creamy dressing. Chopped hard-boiled eggs are delicious mixed into the vinaigrette, as is demerara sugar. A little chilli powder can also be added for piquancy.

5

Desserts

HOT DESSERTS

FRUIT DESSERTS

CHEESECAKE

FRUIT TARTS

MERINGUES

ICED DESSERTS

SAUCES

RICE PUDDING BRULEE

200 g short-grain rice

250 ml water

1 stick cinnamon

Rind of 1 lemon, peeled using a
potato peeler

100 g sugar

Pinch of salt

1 litre full-cream milk

25 g caster sugar

Serves 8

*The contrast of the creamy rice and the sweet, crunchy caramel topping
makes this traditional dessert a special treat.*

1 Place the rice and water in a large saucepan and bring to a boil. Cover
and simmer for 8 minutes until the water is absorbed.

2 Add the cinnamon stick, the lemon rind, the sugar, salt and milk. Bring
back to a boil, then reduce the heat to a very low setting and simmer
gently for 30 minutes, stirring occasionally, until the rice is very
tender and creamy.

3 Remove the cinnamon stick and lemon rind. While still hot, pour the rice
and milk mixture into a 1.5 litre heatproof dish (a soufflé dish is ideal)
or into 8 individual ramekins (approximately 9 cm) and allow to cool. The
rice should fill the containers completely.

4 Once the rice pudding is cold, sprinkle the caster sugar over the top and
place under a very hot grill. Avoid sprinkling the sugar on to the edges
of the dish, as the sugar will burn on to the dish and look untidy. Grill
until the sugar starts to bubble and turn golden, but do not allow to burn.
Once the top of the pudding is caramelized, remove from the heat very
carefully (the dish or ramekins will be very hot) and allow to cool. Serve
as soon as the pudding has cooled – it should not be kept for more than
an hour or so as the caramel topping will begin to soften and dissolve,
losing its crunchy texture.

FRUIT SALAD BRULEE

500 g mixed fresh fruit

150 ml double cream

50 g caster sugar

Serves 6

*The wonderful thing about this dessert is that you can prepare it with
all of your favourite fruits, whether they be the classic, dependable
favourites such as apples, pears, berries and bananas, or more exotic
delicacies such as mango and kiwi fruit.*

1 Chop the fruit into small pieces and spoon equal portions into 6 individual
8.5 cm ramekins, filling them almost to the top.

2 Whip the cream until fairly stiff and, using a spatula, cover the individual
fruit salads with the cream. Smooth out the tops so that the cream is level
with the rims of the ramekins, then sprinkle liberally with sugar.

3 Place under a very hot grill. Make sure that the heat is as high as it can
be, and that you place the ramekins as close to the heat source as possible,
so that the sugar caramelizes quickly, before the cream beneath it melts.
Once caramelized, remove from the heat and allow to cool slightly
before serving.

APRICOT SOUFFLE

Apricots lend a delicate flavour to this classic dessert. The ingredients required for soufflé are general kitchen fare – add a packet of dried apricots to your standard larder contents so that you can always create a last-minute impressive finale to a meal.

1 Preheat the oven to 200°C, gas mark 6. Grease either a 1 litre soufflé dish or 6 individual ramekins (approximately 9 cm) with some melted butter. Dust with icing sugar and set aside.

2 Place the dried apricots in a saucepan and add enough water to just cover them. Bring to a boil and simmer uncovered for 20 minutes, until the fruit is very tender. Drain and allow to cool.

3 Place the apricots in a food processor and purée them. If you do not have a food processor, pass them through a sieve. Blend in the egg yolks and transfer the mixture to a bowl.

4 Whisk the egg whites until stiff, then carefully fold into the apricot mixture. Pour into the prepared soufflé dish and bake in the preheated oven for 20–25 minutes, or for 15 minutes if preparing individual portions. Remove from the oven, dust with icing sugar and serve immediately, with single or double cream, if desired.

Butter for greasing

Icing sugar for dusting

225 g dried apricots

4 eggs, medium-sized, separated

Serves 4–6

HOT FRUIT SALAD

There is no reason why a fruit salad cannot be heated – in fact, a hot fruit salad makes a very satisfying and enjoyable dish on a cold winter's day. Any of your favourite fruits can be used – try those that are seasonably available.

1 Preheat the oven to 200°C, gas mark 6. Grease a shallow ovenproof dish with melted butter.

2 Peel, core and slice the apples. Peel and divide the oranges, removing the pips and any excess pith. Cut the segments in half if too large. Peel and slice the bananas and kiwi fruit.

3 Place the fruit in layers into the prepared dish. Squeeze a little lemon juice over the fruit. Add the sultanas or raisins and dot all over with the butter. Finally, pour over the rum (if using) and sprinkle with the dark brown sugar.

4 Place in the preheated oven for 30 minutes until the fruit is soft but still holds its shape. Serve hot with a scoop of rum and raisin or Vanilla Ice Cream (see page 106), or with Vanilla Custard (see page 108).

2 eating apples

2 oranges

2 bananas

2 kiwi fruit

Juice of I lemon

A few sultanas or raisins

50 g butter, plus extra for greasing

2 tablespoons rum (optional)

2 tablespoons dark brown sugar

Serves 6

PEARS BAKED IN CUSTARD

This recipe is similar to the classic French 'clafoutis' which is usually made with cherries cooked in a light batter. The special ingredient that makes this particular dessert is the almond essence, which infuses the creamy custard with a nutty flavour to complement the sweet and succulent wedges of pear.

1 Preheat the oven to 180°C, gas mark 4. Grease a 12 x 30 cm ovenproof dish with melted butter.

2 Peel, core and slice the pears into wedges. If they are not ripe, poach them gently in a little water with sugar for about 5 minutes to soften them, so that they are just firm, then drain well. Spread the pears over the base of the buttered dish.

3 Beat the eggs with the sugar, almond essence and cornflour. Stir in the cream and mix well.

4 Pour the custard over the pears and then sprinkle the flaked almonds over the top. Place in the oven and cook for approximately 45 minutes until the custard has set. Serve warm with a sprinkling of icing sugar.

Butter for greasing

5–6 ripe pears (according to size)

50 g caster sugar

4 eggs, medium-sized

1 teaspoon almond essence

1 teaspoon cornflour

300 ml double cream

1 tablespoon flaked almonds

Icing sugar to serve

Serves 4–6

APPLES BAKED IN CUSTARD
Eating apples, such as Golden Delicious, can be substituted for the pears in the recipe above. Soften them in butter for about 5 minutes before placing them in the gratin dish with the custard. Mix in 1 tablespoon of Calvados instead of the almond essence, if preferred.

FIGS IN HONEY & WINE

Make this luxurious, yet simple, dessert (see left) during the summer, when figs are plentiful and at their best.

1 Wash the figs and place them in a large saucepan. Pour in enough white wine to cover the fruit, then add the honey.

2 Slowly bring to a boil, then simmer uncovered for approximately 15–20 minutes until the figs are just tender when pierced with a sharp knife. Be careful not to overcook the figs or they will disintegrate.

3 Turn off the heat, leave the figs in the pan and allow to cool and absorb the wine and honey syrup.

4 When cool, place two figs on each plate and serve with a scoop of Vanilla Ice Cream (see page 106) or some Vanilla Custard (see page 108).

8 fresh figs

White wine, approximately ½ bottle

125 ml clear honey

Serves 4

HONEY-POACHED ORANGES

6 small eating oranges

4 tablespoons clear honey

50 g sugar

Juice of 1 lemon

6 whole cloves

1 litre water

Serves 6

Cloves and oranges are a natural combination and here they are poached – and then served – in a delicious honey syrup. The warming cloves and honey contrast with the tang of the oranges.

1   Peel the oranges and remove all the pith. Place the honey, sugar, lemon juice, cloves and water in a saucepan and add the whole oranges.

2   Cook over high heat to boiling point. Then reduce the heat and simmer uncovered for 5–10 minutes, stirring occasionally.

3   Remove the oranges with a slotted spoon and place in a serving bowl. Boil the poaching liquid for 10 minutes to reduce it. Pour the hot syrup over the oranges and cool slightly. Cover and refrigerate for at least 3 hours until chilled before serving.

ORANGE & DATE SALAD

5 large eating oranges

100 g pitted dates, chopped

A little brown sugar (if the oranges are not sweet)

Serves 4–6

This healthy fruit dessert requires very little time to put together and can be prepared well in advance.

1   Peel the oranges and remove all the pith. Divide them into segments and place them in a bowl.

2   Add the chopped dates to the oranges and a little sugar if necessary and stir. Leave to stand for at least an hour before serving so that the dates soften and absorb the orange juice.

ORANGE CREME CARAMEL

FOR THE CARAMEL

125 g sugar

3 tablespoons orange juice

Crème caramel is a traditional family favourite. Here I have flavoured it delicately with fresh orange juice (see right), to give it a boost of added fruitiness.

1   Preheat the oven to 160°C, gas mark 3. Place the sugar and the orange juice in a small saucepan and boil over high heat for approximately 10 minutes, stirring occasionally until the sugar has dissolved and the liquid is thick and golden in colour. Ensure that the syrup does not boil over. Remove from the heat and divide between 6 individual 150 ml crème caramel moulds or pour into the base of one large 800 ml mould.

2   Place the milk (or, for a creamier custard, equal quantities of milk and cream) in a saucepan with the orange rind. Cook over low heat and bring to just below boiling point.

3   Beat the eggs and the sugar in a bowl or jug – a jug is best for pouring the custard into the moulds later. While still beating, gradually add the hot milk to the egg mixture.

4   Pour the custard carefully on to the caramel in the moulds and sit the moulds in a roasting tin which is half full of hot (but not boiling) water. The water should be roughly at a level with the middle of the moulds. Place the roasting tin containing the filled moulds in the preheated oven for approximately 1 hour if using a large mould, or for 45 minutes if using individual moulds. To make sure the custard has set, insert a knife into it and if it comes out clean, the custard is ready.

5   Allow to cool. For best results, refrigerate for at least 24 hours before serving, giving the caramel at the bottom of the moulds time to dissolve slightly, thereby producing more syrup. To serve, carefully loosen the custard from the mould with a knife and turn out. Serve on its own, with single cream or Orange Syrup (see page 115).

FOR THE CUSTARD

500 ml milk or 250 ml milk and 250 ml cream

Grated rind of 1 orange

4 large eggs

50 g sugar

Serves 6

VANILLA CHEESECAKE

Light and refreshing, cheesecake is a classic favourite that never fails to please (see left). This basic recipe is delicious alone, but for a special occasion, give it a raspberry topping for a really luxurious flavour.

1   Preheat the oven to 160°C, gas mark 3. Using melted butter, grease a 20 cm spring-form cake tin.

2   To make the base crust, place the cornflakes, sugar and melted butter in a food processor and process until fairly fine, or place in a plastic bag and crush with a rolling pin. Place in the bottom of the prepared tin and press down with a metal spoon to create an even layer.

3   To make the filling, first rub the cottage cheese (or ricotta) through a sieve into a bowl. Separate the eggs, putting the whites and yolks into different bowls.

4   Mix the sugar and cornflour together and add to the egg yolks. Beat until light and creamy. Work in the cheese, blending it in well. Then add the vanilla extract and soured cream. Mix everything together thoroughly.

5   Whisk the egg whites until stiff, then carefully fold into the egg and cheese mixture.

6   Pour the cheesecake mixture over the base crust in the cake tin and bake in the preheated oven for 1 hour, until the filling has set. Turn off the heat but leave the cheesecake in the oven until it cools. When cold, chill the cheesecake for 24 hours before serving or topping.

FOR THE BASE CRUST

Butter for greasing

100 g cornflakes

50 g caster sugar

50 g butter, melted

FOR THE FILLING

500 g cottage cheese (or ricotta cheese)

3 large eggs

100 g caster sugar

25 g cornflour

1 teaspoon vanilla extract

150 ml soured cream

Serves 6–8

RASPBERRY GLAZE TOPPING

Clean 500 g of fresh raspberries. Set aside half of them to decorate the top of the cheesecake. Make a purée with the rest of the berries, either by blending in a food processor or passing through a sieve.

Place the purée in a saucepan and add 50 g of caster sugar. Set over low heat and cook gently to draw out the juice. Meanwhile, mix 1 tablespoon of cornflour with 3 tablespoons of water and add to the raspberries in the saucepan. Bring to a boil and stir until thickened. Cook for 1–2 minutes, then add a knob of butter and stir until melted. Strain the purée and leave to cool.

Spoon the glaze over the cheesecake, decorate with the whole raspberries and chill until ready to serve.

PINEAPPLE GLAZE TOPPING

Use pineapple as an alternative to a berry topping for cheesecake. Drain a 450 g can of crushed pineapple to leave approximately 200 g of fruit. Place this in a pan and add 50 g of caster sugar, 1 tablespoon of cornflour and a knob of butter. Cook as for Raspberry Glaze Topping, above.

APPLE TART

FOR THE SHORTCRUST PASTRY

150 g maize meal (or cornmeal)

50 g butter, chilled and cut into pieces

3 teaspoons caster sugar

1 egg, medium-sized, beaten

FOR THE APPLE FILLING

4 large eating apples (such as Golden Delicious)

50 g butter

50 g sugar

Juice of 1 lemon

225 g apricot jam

Serves 6

When making pastry, an excellent gluten-free alternative to conventional flour is maize meal. This recipe for apple tart uses eating apples rather than cooking apples for a softer, more delicate flavour. The pastry shell does not need to be baked blind (part-baked) before being filled. An apricot glaze will give the tart an attractive finish.

1   Preheat the oven to 180°C, gas mark 4. Process the maize meal, butter and sugar in a food processor. Alternatively, place the flour and sugar in a mixing bowl and rub in the butter with your fingertips until the mixture has a crumbly texture, similar to that of breadcrumbs.

2   Once the maize meal and butter are well blended, add the beaten egg and mix it in with a palate knife to make a dough. If the pastry is too dry and crumbly, add a drop or two of water to help it hold together. Make a ball with the pastry using your hands.

3   Place the ball of pastry between two lengths of clingfilm and carefully flatten it with a rolling pin until you have a fairly even sheet of pastry that is large enough to line a 25 cm flan or tart tin. Use a tin that has a removable base.

4   Take off the top piece of clingfilm and, using the bottom piece to help you, lift up the pastry and turn it over into the tin. There is no need to grease the tin first, as the pastry is oily enough itself. Remove the clingfilm and press the pastry into the tin. Work the dough up the sides of the tin, cutting off any excess pastry and patching up where necessary. Try to handle the pastry as little as possible to stop it becoming sticky.

5   To make the filling, peel, quarter and core the apples and slice them fairly thinly and evenly. Melt the butter in a large frying pan and place the sliced apples in it with the sugar and lemon juice. Cook gently for approximately 10 minutes, until the apples begin to soften. Turn the slices over from time to time and shake the pan to ensure that all the apples are evenly cooked. Try not to break them or brown them.

6   Remove the cooked apples from the pan and place them in the pastry case. Arrange them attractively, in overlapping circles, for example. Set aside the buttery juices.

7   Place the tart on a baking sheet and bake in the preheated oven for 25–30 minutes until the edges of the crust are golden brown. Take out of the oven, remove the outer rim of the tin and pour over the reserved buttery juices.

8   To make apricot glaze, place some apricot jam in a small saucepan and cook over low heat until runny. Strain out the fruit. Pour the remaining syrup over the apple tart. Serve warm or cold with cream or ice cream.

LEMON CUSTARD TART

The clean, refreshing taste of this tart (see above) makes it ideal for serving after a heavy meal. This recipe works just as well using limes, in which case you will need three pieces of fruit.

1 Preheat the oven to 180°C, gas mark 4. Prepare the shortcrust pastry as for Apple Tart (see opposite) and mould it into a 25 cm flan or tart tin. Line the tart shell loosely with foil and fill with dried beans, uncooked rice or ceramic baking beans (alternatively, make a few incisions in the base using a sharp knife) and place in the oven to bake blind for 15 minutes. Remove from the oven, discard the foil and beans (if using) and leave to cool.

2 Place the eggs and sugar in a food processor and blend thoroughly. Or put in a bowl and beat with a hand-whisk until fairly creamy. Add the grated lemon rind and lemon juice to the egg and sugar mixture. Stir to combine all the ingredients, then add the double cream and mix well.

3 Pour this mixture into the partly-baked pastry shell, then place it on a baking tin and return to the oven for another 25–30 minutes until the custard has set. Remove from the oven and allow to cool completely, then remove the outer rim of the tin and place on a plate. Sprinkle with icing sugar and serve either alone or with whipped cream. For an attractive presentation, cut paper strips of the same size and place them on the tart, overlapping them to make a pattern of your choice, such as the diamond pattern shown above. Dust with icing sugar, then remove the paper strips carefully to reveal the pattern.

25 cm shortcrust pastry case as for Apple Tart (see opposite)

4 eggs, medium-sized

125 g caster sugar

Grated rind and juice of 2 lemons

200 ml double cream

Icing sugar for dusting

Serves 6

Almond Meringue Gateau

Corn oil for greasing

4 egg whites

225 g caster sugar

`1 teaspoon cornflour

2 teaspoons vanilla extract

½ teaspoon white wine vinegar

100 g ground almonds

250 ml double cream

Icing sugar for dusting

8 whole unblanched almonds

Raspberry or Strawberry Coulis to serve
(see page 109)

Serves 6

This simple but divine meringue gâteau (see below) can also be made using ground hazelnuts. Serve it with a raspberry or strawberry coulis.

1 Preheat the oven to 190°C, gas mark 5. Grease two 20 cm loose-based sandwich tins with corn oil and line the bases with baking parchment.

2 Make a meringue with the egg whites and sugar (see opposite page). Quickly whisk the cornflour, vanilla extract and vinegar into the meringue, then gently fold in the ground nuts. Divide evenly and spoon into the prepared tins. Bake in the centre of the oven for 35 minutes.

3 Remove from the oven and allow the meringues to cool in the tins. Once cool, carefully turn them out, running a palette knife around the edge of the meringues to loosen them from the tin, if necessary. Remove the lining.

4 Whisk the cream until thick, not buttery. Place one of the meringues on a cake stand and spread the whipped cream evenly over the top. Place the other meringue gently on top of the cream. Sift icing sugar over the gâteau, decorate with almonds and serve with a fresh Fruit Coulis (see page 109).

MAKING MERINGUE

Place 4 egg whites in a large, clean mixing bowl and whisk until stiff. Then whisk in 225 g caster sugar, adding 1 tablespoon of sugar at a time. Whisk the mixture well between each addition.

MAKING MERINGUE NESTS

To make meringue nests, preheat the oven to 100°C, gas mark ¼. Fill a large piping bag (fitted with a medium-sized star nozzle) with meringue mixture (see above). Line two baking sheets with parchment. Draw eight 14 cm circles on the paper with a pencil, turn the paper over and pipe a continuous spiral of meringue to fill each circle, starting in the centre. Pipe a second layer on the edge of each circle to form a wall. Bake for 4–5 hours. Turn off the oven but leave the nests inside until cold. Store in an airtight container for up to 3 weeks. Fill the nests with whipped cream and fruit or Vanilla Ice Cream (see page 106) drizzled with a Fruit Coulis (page 109) or Chocolate Sauce (page 109).

ROLLED COCONUT MERINGUE

This spectacular dessert is easier to make than it appears. Although any creamy filling can be used, a mixture of tangy home-made lemon curd and cream contrasts well with the sweet meringue. Alternatively, the cream can be flavoured with melted chocolate, coffee liqueur or Strawberry Coulis (see page 109).

4 egg whites
225 g caster sugar
2 level tablespoons cornflour
2 teaspoons vanilla extract
1 teaspoon white wine vinegar
115 g desiccated coconut
125 ml double cream
125 ml home-made Lemon Curd (see page 108)
Icing sugar for dusting
Serves 6–8

1   Preheat the oven to 140°C, gas mark 1. Line a 23 x 28 cm swiss roll tin with baking parchment.

2   Prepare the meringues using the egg whites and sugar (see above). Quickly whisk in the cornflour, vanilla extract and vinegar, then carefully fold in the desiccated coconut.

3   Spread the meringue evenly over the prepared tin and bake in the centre of the oven for 40 minutes. Remove from the oven, cover with a clean, damp tea towel and leave to cool in the tin.

4   Pour the cream into a chilled bowl and whisk until thick (but not buttery), then fold in the lemon curd.

5   Cut a sheet of baking parchment slightly larger than the tin used to bake the meringue. Lay it on a work surface, then turn the cooled meringue out on to the paper. Peel off the paper that originally lined the tin. Spread the lemon cream evenly over the meringue and roll it up from one of the short ends, using the baking parchment beneath it to help you push the roll along. Do not worry if it cracks a little, as it will be delicious anyhow.

6   Transfer the rolled meringue to a serving dish. Cover it loosely with foil and chill until ready to serve. Dust lightly with icing sugar.

VANILLA ICE CREAM

Serve this simple vanilla ice cream with a rich chocolate or fruity sauce, or as an accompaniment to fruit tarts, crumbles and pies.

3 eggs, separated

50 g sugar

200 ml double cream

1 teaspoon vanilla extract

Serves 6

1 Put the egg yolks and sugar in a bowl with 2 tablespoons of water and place over a saucepan of simmering water – this allows the mixture to be surrounded by a gentle heat, which will heat it through slowly, helping to prevent it curdling. Stir until the mixture begins to thicken to a consistency that will coat the back of a spoon. Remove the custard from the heat and continue stirring until cooled.

2 Beat the egg whites in a bowl until stiff. In a separate bowl, beat the double cream until thick, then stir in the vanilla extract.

3 Fold the cooled custard into the cream, then carefully fold in the egg whites. Pour this ice cream mixture into a 1 litre loaf tin or plastic box, cover and freeze.

4 When ready to serve, run a sharp knife around the container and turn the ice cream out of the mould on to a serving platter. Slice the ice cream and serve each slice with a generous helping of Chocolate Sauce (see page 109) or Raspberry Sauce (see below).

CHOCOLATE CHIP ICE CREAM WITH RASPBERRY SAUCE

The flecks of chocolate in this recipe work remarkably well with a luscious raspberry sauce.

FOR THE ICE CREAM

3 egg whites

125 g caster sugar

250 ml double cream

100 g plain chocolate, grated

1 teaspoon vanilla extract

FOR THE RASPBERRY SAUCE

250 g raspberries, fresh or frozen

Caster sugar to taste

2 tablespoons cassis liqueur (optional)

Serves 6

1 Beat the egg whites in a bowl until stiff. Gradually add half the sugar, a little at a time, beating continuously until the mixture is stiff and glossy.

2 In a separate bowl, whip the cream until thick, gradually adding the rest of the sugar, the grated chocolate and the vanilla extract.

3 Fold the egg white mixture into the whipped cream and chocolate. Pour into a 1 litre loaf tin or plastic box, cover and freeze.

4 Meanwhile, place the raspberries in a food processor and blend into a purée, then sieve to remove the seeds. (If you do not have a food processor, just pass the raspberries through a sieve.) Add a little sugar to taste and stir in the cassis liqueur, if using.

5 Run a sharp knife around the edge of the container and turn out the ice cream. Cut into slices and serve drizzled generously with raspberry sauce.

STRAWBERRY SORBET

Besides being wonderfully refreshing, sorbet is very easily made, as it is simply iced sugared water which is given body with beaten egg whites and flavour with a fruit coulis or purée.

1   Rub the prepared strawberries through a nylon sieve into a bowl to make a purée. Place the sugar and water in a saucepan and boil for 5 minutes to make a syrup. Allow to cool completely, then pour the syrup into the fruit purée and mix well. Place the mixture in a plastic box in the freezer for 1–2 hours until half frozen.

2   Remove the sorbet mixture from the freezer and beat until smooth. Fold in the stiffly beaten egg whites and return to the freezer for a further 1–2 hours until fairly hard. Serve directly from the freezer.

500 g strawberries, washed and hulled

50 g sugar

150 ml water

2 egg whites, stiffly beaten

Serves 4–6

COFFEE PRALINE MOUSSE

Praline provides a crunchy topping to contrast with the smooth texture of this tempting coffee mousse.

1   Place the milk in a saucepan and heat over medium heat without bringing to a boil. When the milk is steaming, stir in the instant coffee. Beat the egg yolks and sugar in a mixing bowl until thick and creamy, then gradually add the flavoured milk. Return to the pan and stir continuously over low heat until the custard thickens – it should coat the back of a wooden spoon. Do not allow the mixture to boil or it will curdle. Leave to cool.

2   Dissolve the gelatine in 3 tablespoons of hot water in a small saucepan. Stir vigorously and allow to stand for 1–2 minutes. If not completely dissolved, place over very low heat for a few seconds and stir. Do not allow the liquid to boil. Once transparent and runny, stir a little of the custard mixture into the gelatine, then pour it back into the remaining custard. Stir well and allow to cool completely and begin to set – place it in the refrigerator to accelerate the process. Ensure it does not set completely.

3   Whip the cream a little and fold into the custard. In a separate bowl, whisk the egg whites until stiff. Then carefully fold these into the mixture. Pour the mousse into a 1 litre mould or soufflé dish and refrigerate for at least 2 hours. When ready to serve, sprinkle liberally with the praline.

500 ml milk

30 g (or 2 tablespoons) instant coffee

3 eggs, medium-sized, separated

75 g caster sugar

1 tablespoon (or 1 envelope) powdered gelatine

100 ml double cream

Serves 6

MAKING PRALINE

Place 100 g of granulated sugar and 1 tablespoon of water in a saucepan and heat gently until dissolved. Boil until golden then stir in 100 g of toasted almond flakes. Turn the mixture out on to an oiled baking sheet to cool, then crush with a pestle in a mortar or blend in a food processor until crumbly.

Lemon Curd

225 g sugar

Grated rind and juice of 2 lemons

75 g butter, cut into pieces

3 eggs

Makes approximately 450 g

There are many uses for this tart, creamy lemon sauce – for instance, as a topping for baked desserts or, for a simple pudding, as a filling for a pastry case, along with some fresh whipped cream.

1 Place the sugar in a bowl over a small saucepan of simmering water and add the lemon juice and rind. Stir the mixture occasionally as it slowly heats until the sugar has dissolved completely. Stir in the pieces of butter until they have melted and are fully blended with the sugar and lemon. Remove from the heat and leave to cool.

2 Beat the eggs in a separate bowl and pour the cooled lemon and sugar mixture on to them. Strain and place over the pan of simmering water. Cook over this gentle heat and stir until the lemon curd is thick enough to coat the back of a wooden spoon.

3 Remove from the heat and pour the lemon curd into warmed clean jars. Leave to cool and thicken for 24 hours. Lemon curd will keep for 1–2 weeks if refrigerated in an airtight container.

Vanilla Custard

500 ml milk, plus 2 tablespoons extra for mixing with the cornflour

2 teaspoons cornflour

25 g caster sugar

2 eggs

1 teaspoon vanilla extract

Makes 600 ml

This rich custard is warming and filling and delicious served with stewed fruits, pies and crumbles.

1 Pour the milk into a saucepan and heat over low heat until the milk is hot, but not boiling.

2 Blend the cornflour with a little cold milk, then stir this mixture into the hot milk. (The cornflour stabilises the custard, making it less likely to curdle.) Slowly bring to a boil and cook for a few seconds. Remove the pan from the heat and stir in the sugar. Leave to cool, stirring occasionally.

3 Beat the eggs in a bowl. Stir in some of the milk and cornflour mixture, then pour back into the saucepan with the remaining milk. Heat gently, stirring constantly, until the custard reaches the right consistency to coat the back of a wooden spoon. Do not boil the mixture.

4 Remove from the heat, stir in the vanilla extract and allow to cool a little, stirring continuously to prevent a skin from forming on the top.

5 Use immediately. Vanilla custard makes an excellent accompaniment to Apple Tart (see page 102) or Hot Fruit Salad (see page 95).

FRUIT COULIS

A coulis is a puréed sauce which is either savoury or sweet (above, left and front are a strawberry and a raspberry coulis). The consistency should be pourable. For a fresh fruit coulis, process the cleaned fruit in a blender and strain out the pips or fibres if necessary (as with raspberries, for instance). Add sugar, lemon juice and liqueur for extra flavour, if desired.

DRIED APRICOT PUREE

To make apricot purée (above, right), soak 250 g of dried apricots in water for a few hours, then drain and cook in 500 ml of water for 20 minutes until soft. Allow to cool a little, then purée with the cooking liquid, adding a little more water if necessary. Sugar should not be needed, but can be added if desired.

CHOCOLATE SAUCE

Put 200 g of chopped plain chocolate in a bowl and place over a saucepan of simmering water, ensuring the bowl does not touch the water in the pan. Heat gently until the chocolate has melted. Add double or single cream to make the sauce richer. For extra flavour, add orange juice or a liqueur.

6

Cakes &
Breads

CHOCOLATE CAKES

SPONGE CAKES

MUFFINS

TEACAKES

BREADS

CHOCOLATE HAZELNUT CAKE

This decadent, rich and moist pudding-like cake (see left) will keep well for several days if stored in an airtight container. It can be made using ground almonds in place of the hazelnuts.

1 Preheat the oven to 180°C, gas mark 4. Butter a 25 cm spring-form cake tin and line the base with non-stick baking parchment.

2 Place 300 g of the chocolate into a medium-sized mixing bowl and stand this over a saucepan of gently simmering water. Stir until the chocolate has melted. Add 175 g of the butter, stir until evenly blended with the chocolate, then remove from the heat.

3 Put the egg yolks and sugar in a large mixing bowl and whisk until thick and creamy. Stir in the yogurt and hazelnuts, then add the melted chocolate and butter and mix well.

4 Whisk the egg whites until stiff. Fold a quarter into the chocolate mixture to loosen it a little, then gently fold in the rest.

5 Pour the mixture into the prepared tin and bake in the centre of the oven for 60–70 minutes until the cake is well risen and feels firm to the touch. Use the skewer test (see opposite) to ensure the cake is cooked through. Leave to cool in the tin.

6 When the cake is cold, run a palette knife around the side to loosen it from the edges of the tin. Remove the cake from the tin, carefully transfer it on to a serving plate and peel off the lining paper.

7 Melt the remaining chocolate in a small bowl that is standing over a saucepan of simmering water and stir in the remaining butter.

8 Spread the chocolate icing over the top of the cake with a palette knife and mark it into swirls. Once the icing has set, cut the cake into slices and serve with single cream poured over it.

FOR THE CAKE

300 g good quality dark chocolate, roughly chopped

175 g unsalted butter, cut into small cubes, plus extra for greasing

6 eggs, medium-sized, separated

115 g soft dark brown sugar

125 ml plain yogurt

250 g ground hazelnuts

Single cream to serve (optional)

FOR THE CHOCOLATE ICING

100 g good quality dark chocolate, roughly chopped

25 g unsalted butter, cut into small cubes, plus extra for greasing

Serves 6–8

BUTTER ICING

If you prefer a less chocolatey topping, try a simple butter icing. To make this, beat 50 g of butter with a wooden spoon until light and fluffy. Gradually sift in 50–75 g of icing sugar until the desired texture and level of sweetness are achieved. Spread the butter icing over the cake and decorate with grated chocolate. This recipe produces enough icing to cover a 20 cm cake.

Chocolate Hazelnut Cake is delicious with orange or coffee icing, both of which can be made by flavouring the basic butter icing recipe given here. For orange icing, blend 1 teaspoon of finely grated orange rind with 1 tablespoon of orange juice and mix into the icing. For coffee flavour, dissolve 1 teaspoon of instant coffee in 1 tablespoon of hot water and mix into the icing.

CHOCOLATE ROULADE

For the best results, the chocolate sponge for this roulade should be made the day before, but it can be used sooner, so long as it is left to stand for at least two hours after baking.

1 Preheat the oven to 190°C, gas mark 5. Line a 25 x 35 cm swiss roll tin with baking parchment, allowing the paper to sit a little above the sides of the tin. Cut a second sheet of parchment to the same size and set aside.

2 Place the pieces of chocolate in a bowl sitting over a saucepan of gently simmering water. Stir until the chocolate melts. Mix in 3 tablespoons of hot water – if the chocolate becomes lumpy, continue stirring until smooth.

3 Place the egg yolks in a large mixing bowl and whisk with the sugar until light and fluffy. Gradually whisk in the melted chocolate.

4 Beat the egg whites until soft peaks form. Fold a quarter of this into the chocolate mixture to loosen it a little, then carefully fold in the remainder. Pour the mixture into the prepared tin and spread it evenly into all four corners. Bake in the centre of the preheated oven for 20 minutes or until well risen and firm to the touch.

5 Grease one side of the reserved sheet of parchment. Remove the cooked sponge from the oven and immediately cover the top with the parchment, buttered-side down. Cover with a clean, damp tea towel and leave to stand for a few hours or until the next day.

6 Uncover the swiss roll tin, remove the top sheet of parchment and set aside. Sift lightly with icing sugar, cover with the parchment and, holding the sponge firmly between parchment and tin, turn the tin upside-down on to the work surface. Remove the tin and peel off the lining paper.

7 Pour the cream into a chilled bowl, add the vanilla extract and whisk until thick, but not buttery. Spread the whipped cream evenly over the sponge and roll it up, starting at a short end. Use the parchment beneath the sponge to help you push the roll along. Do not worry if the sponge cracks a little as you roll it – this is normal. Once rolled up, dust the roulade with icing sugar – this helps to cover any imperfections on the surface.

8 Carefully lift the roulade on to a board. Loosely cover with foil and chill for 2 hours before serving with a freshly-made Raspberry or Strawberry Coulis (see page 109).

150 g good quality dark chocolate, roughly chopped

4 eggs, medium-sized, separated

115 g caster sugar

Butter for greasing

Icing sugar for dusting

200 ml double cream

½ teaspoon vanilla extract

Raspberry or Strawberry Coulis (see page 109) to serve (optional)

Serves 8

THE SKEWER TEST
To test if a cake is cooked through, pierce it to the centre with a skewer. If the skewer comes out clean and dry, the cake is ready. If not, the cake should be cooked for a little longer.

CHOCOLATE WALNUT CAKE

The delightfully gooey texture of this cake is very much like that of brownies. The nuts provide richness and flavour.

Butter for greasing

250 g ground walnuts

250 g unsweetened cocoa powder

5 eggs, medium-sized

250 g caster sugar

Icing sugar for dusting

Serves 6–8

1 Preheat the oven to 190°C, gas mark 5. Grease and line the base of a 20 cm non-stick sandwich tin which has a removable base.

2 Mix the ground walnuts and cocoa powder with two of the eggs. Once you have a stiff paste, mix in the remaining three eggs, one at a time. Slowly work in the sugar, making sure that everything is well-mixed.

3 Spoon the cake mixture into the buttered and lined sandwich tin. Place the tin in the preheated oven and bake for approximately 60 minutes. Towards the end of the cooking time, use the skewer test (see page 113) to ensure the cake is cooked through. Cool a little, turn out on to a wire rack and remove the lining paper.

4 Dust with icing sugar. Serve this cake alone as a tea-time snack, or with single cream or Vanilla Ice Cream (see page 106) as a dessert.

LEMON POLENTA & ALMOND CAKE

Polenta gives this lemon and almond cake an unusual and delightfully crunchy texture. The lemon juice and rind provide a hint of sharpness that complements the earthy flavour of the almonds.

220 g butter, slightly salted, plus extra for greasing

220 g caster sugar

4 eggs, medium-sized

200 g ground almonds

1 teaspoon vanilla extract

150 g fine grain polenta

Grated rind and juice of 1 lemon

1 teaspoon gluten-free baking powder

Serves 6–8

1 Preheat the oven to 190°C, gas mark 5. Use melted butter to grease a 20 cm non-stick cake tin which has a removable base. It is also advisable to line the base with a circle of greaseproof paper, cut to size and greased with melted butter.

2 Beat the butter with the sugar in a mixing bowl until light and creamy. Then gradually beat in the eggs, one at a time.

3 Stir in the ground almonds and vanilla extract until they are thoroughly combined with the sugar, butter and egg mixture, then fold in the polenta, lemon rind and juice and the baking powder.

4 Spoon the cake mixture into the prepared cake tin and place in the preheated oven. Bake for 60–70 minutes. Use the skewer test (see page 113) to ensure the cake is cooked through – it should feel moist to the touch and be fairly brown on the top surface. Serve Lemon Polenta and Almond cake alone, or with a generous spoonful of mascarpone cheese.

ALMOND SPONGE CAKE

This light, moist sponge cake (see above) is easy to make and its flavour is gloriously complemented by the tangy orange syrup.

1 Preheat the oven to 180°C, gas mark 4. Use melted butter to grease a 20 cm non-stick cake tin with a removable base. Cut a circle of greaseproof paper to fit the base, place it in the tin and grease with butter.

2 Whisk the egg yolks with the sugar until light and creamy. Then slowly fold in the ground almonds and lemon rind. Beat the egg whites until stiff and stir a little of this into the yolk and sugar mixture to soften it, then gently fold in the rest.

3 Pour the cake mixture into the prepared cake tin and bake in the preheated oven for approximately 40 minutes. Use the skewer test (see page 113) to ensure the cake is cooked through.

4 When the cake is cooked, remove it from the oven and leave to cool. Pass a knife around the edge of the cake to loosen it from the sides of the tin, then turn out on to a plate and remove the lining paper. Make a few deep holes in the top of the cake with a skewer.

5 To make the orange syrup, place the orange juice, sugar and cinnamon stick in a saucepan and simmer for 5–6 minutes, allowing the sugar to dissolve. Leave to cool, then pour over the cake – the syrup is absorbed through the holes. Top the cake with the cinnamon stick for decoration.

FOR THE CAKE

Butter for greasing

5 eggs, separated

175 g caster sugar

175 g ground almonds

Grated rind of 1 lemon

FOR THE ORANGE SYRUP

Juice of 2 oranges

50 g sugar

1 stick cinnamon

Serves 6–8

ORANGE & ALMOND CAKE

Because it is made with fresh whole oranges, this soft, pudding-like cake (see left) has a wonderfully strong citrus flavour.

Butter for greasing
2 large oranges
6 eggs, medium-sized, separated
250 g caster sugar
225 g ground almonds
Serves 6–8

1 Preheat the oven to 180°C, gas mark 4. Grease a 23 cm non-stick cake tin which has a removable base. Cut a circle of parchment to fit the base, grease it with melted butter and use to line the base.

2 Place the whole, unpeeled oranges into a saucepan of water and boil for 2 hours until completely soft. Alternatively, cook them in a pressure cooker for half an hour.

3 Remove from the pan and cool slightly. Then cut them open and remove the pips. Place the oranges in a food processor and blend with the egg yolks. Alternatively, mash the oranges with a fork and whisk with the egg yolks in a mixing bowl.

4 Add the sugar and ground almonds to the orange and egg mixture, a little at a time, and continue blending until all the ingredients are well-combined. Transfer to a large bowl.

5 Beat the egg whites until stiff in a separate bowl. Now fold these carefully into the orange mixture.

6 Pour the cake mixture into the prepared tin and bake in the preheated oven for 60–70 minutes. Use the skewer test (see page 113) to ensure the cake is cooked through. When cooked, remove from the oven and allow to cool before turning out.

7 Run a knife around the edge of the cake to loosen it from the sides of the tin, turn out on to a plate and remove the lining paper. The cake may be iced with orange flavoured Butter Icing (see page 112) or Marmalade Sauce (see below), or served with crème fraîche, mascarpone cheese or fresh strawberries.

MARMALADE SAUCE

This is the ideal topping for Orange and Almond cake. To make it, mix 150 g of fine-cut orange marmalade with 200 ml of orange juice (which is the juice of roughly 2 oranges) in a saucepan. Place the pan over medium heat and bring the liquid to a boil, stirring constantly to ensure the marmalade dissolves and mixes with the orange juice. Remove the pan from the heat. Mix 2 tablespoons of arrowroot with 2 tablespoons of water in a cup and stir this into the hot orange liquid. Reheat gently, stirring constantly until the sauce thickens. If preferred, the orange peel can be removed using a sieve. Consume the sauce either hot or cold. This recipe makes approximately 300 ml of sauce.

For a rich and creamy sauce, strain out the peel, allow to cool, then mix in 2 tablespoons of single cream.

DATE & BROWN SUGAR MUFFINS

50 g butter (or margarine), plus extra for greasing

50 g soft dark brown sugar, plus extra for sprinkling

2 eggs, medium-sized

200 ml buttermilk

100 g maize meal (or cornmeal)

100 g brown rice flour

1 rounded teaspoon gluten-free baking powder

50 g dates, stoned and chopped

Makes 6 large (or 12 small) muffins

These tempting muffins (see right) are ideal served with afternoon tea, but are just as good for a sweet and fruity breakfast.

1 Preheat the oven to 200°C, gas mark 6. Use a little butter to grease a 100 ml 6-hole muffin tin. (If you prefer smaller muffins, use a 12-hole muffin tin instead.)

2 Using a wooden spoon, beat together the butter (or margarine) and sugar until light and creamy. Beat in the eggs one at a time, then, once they are thoroughly blended with the butter and sugar, stir in the buttermilk. (Ordinary milk, soured with a squeeze of lemon juice, may be used in place of the buttermilk.)

3 Mix the maize meal, rice flour and baking powder in a separate bowl, then gradually fold this into the butter, eggs and buttermilk mixture. Finally, add the chopped dates.

4 Divide the mixture into 6 (or 12) portions and spoon these evenly into the greased muffin tin. Sprinkle the tops of each portion with a little brown sugar.

5 Place the muffin tin on a baking tin and put in the top half of the preheated oven. Bake the muffins for 25–30 minutes (or for 20 minutes if making smaller muffins). Test the muffins using the skewer test (see page 113) to determine whether or not they are cooked through. Remove them from the oven when thoroughly cooked and allow to cool in the tin. Turn out on to a wire rack and serve fresh – just cooled – cut in half and spread with butter.

BANANA MUFFINS
Add 1 very ripe mashed banana to the basic batter in place of the dates to make tasty and fragrant banana muffins.

RAISIN OR APRICOT MUFFINS
Use 50 g of seedless raisins in place of the dates for fruity raisin muffins. Other ready-to-eat dried fruits, such as apricots, can also be used. These should be chopped very finely.

SAVOURY CHEESE MUFFINS
The basic muffin recipe given above can be used to make delicious savoury muffins. Follow the steps above but omit the sugar and dates. Instead, beat the butter with 50 g of grated Parmesan cheese and season the mixture with plenty of freshly ground black pepper. Do not add salt, as the cheese is salty enough. Add this mixture to the basic muffin batter, then sprinkle the tops of the muffins with a little more grated Parmesan cheese before baking them as for the sweet muffins, above.

FRUIT & NUT LOAF

Butter for greasing

200 g margarine

200 g sugar

4 eggs, medium-sized

200 g maize meal (or cornmeal)

1 teaspoon gluten-free baking powder

1 teaspoon cinnamon

50 g chopped nuts (any type)

50 g seeded raisins

Serves 6–8

Maize meal is readily available in supermarkets and can be used to make delicious teacakes, such as this fruit and nut loaf (see below), which keeps well for several days.

1 Preheat the oven to 180°C, gas mark 4. Using butter and baking parchment, grease and line a 11 x 21 cm non-stick loaf tin.

2 Beat the margarine with a wooden spoon in a bowl until light and creamy. Add the sugar and continue beating, then beat in the eggs, one at a time.

3 Work in the maize meal, baking powder and cinnamon. Once all of the ingredients are combined, add the nuts and raisins.

4 Spoon the mixture into the greased and lined loaf tin and gently even out the batter. Place in the preheated oven and bake for 60 minutes. Use the skewer test (see page 113) to ensure the cake is thoroughly cooked.

5 Allow to cool, then run a knife around the edge of the loaf to loosen it from the tin. Turn out and cut into slices to serve, alone or with butter.

SAND CAKE

This cake has a dry, compact texture which may be complemented by a fruit compote or creamy fruit dessert. Alternatively, serve it alone as a teacake. The taste of sandcake improves with standing – after making it, wait for a day to allow the flavours to mature.

200 g butter, plus extra for greasing
175 g caster sugar
3 eggs, separated
50 g ground almonds
Grated rind and juice of ½ lemon
200 g cornflour
Serves 6–8

1   Preheat the oven to 180°C, gas mark 4. Grease a 20 cm non-stick sponge tin or square cake tin with melted butter.

2   Beat the butter and sugar together with a wooden spoon in a mixing bowl until light and creamy. Add the egg yolks one at a time, until all the ingredients are thoroughly blended. Mix in the ground almonds, the lemon rind and juice and finally, the cornflour.

3   Beat the egg whites until stiff and forming soft peaks. Add a little of this to the cake mixture to soften it. Carefully fold in the remaining egg whites with a large metal spoon.

4   Spoon the mixture into the prepared tin and bake in the preheated oven for 50–60 minutes. Test that the cake is cooked using the skewer test (see page 113).

5   When cooked, remove from the oven and allow to cool slightly. Then turn out on to a wire rack and serve.

RICE CAKE

Rice cake has a wonderful creamy flavour and soft texture. Serve slices or wedges with a Fruit Coulis (see page 109).

100 g short-grain rice (or pudding rice)
½ litre milk
Pinch of salt
50 g butter, plus extra for greasing
Grated rind of ½ lemon
75 g caster sugar
3 eggs, medium-sized, separated
Icing sugar for dusting
Serves 6–8

1   Place the rice in the milk with a pinch of salt. Heat to simmer and cook for approximately 30 minutes, until the rice is soft and has absorbed all of the milk. Stir and allow to cool a little.

2   Preheat the oven to 180°C, gas mark 4. Grease a 20 cm spring-form cake tin with butter and line the base with baking parchment.

3   Beat the butter and sugar together until light and creamy. Add the egg yolks one at a time, then stir in the cooked rice and mix well until fully blended. Whisk the egg whites until stiff, then fold them into the mixture.

4   Pour the mixture into the greased cake tin and bake in the preheated oven for 45–50 minutes until cooked through. Test that the cake is cooked using the skewer test (see page 113). Once cooked, remove from the oven and allow to cool slightly. Run a knife around the edge of the tin and turn out the cake. Dust with icing sugar when ready to serve.

HERB & OLIVE BREAD

4 tablespoons light olive oil, plus
extra for greasing

200 g maize meal (or cornmeal)

100 g brown rice flour

1 teaspoon gluten-free baking powder

1 teaspoon dried mixed herbs

1 teaspoon salt

4 eggs, medium-sized

250 ml buttermilk (or plain yogurt)

100 g pitted green olives, chopped

Serves 6–8

Herb and olive bread makes a satisfying snack when served, either plain or toasted, with slices of cheese and cold meats. For a light meal, add a leafy salad and tangy vinaigrette which can be soaked up by the bread.

1 Preheat the oven to 180°C, gas mark 4. Grease an 11 x 21 cm non-stick loaf tin with a little oil and line with baking parchment.

2 Mix the maize meal, rice flour, baking powder, dried herbs and salt in a large bowl.

3 Whisk the eggs in a bowl, then add the buttermilk (or plain yogurt) and olive oil and mix well.

4 Pour the egg mixture on to the flour mixture and stir with a wooden spoon until thoroughly combined. Finally, add the chopped olives.

5 Spoon the loaf mixture into the oiled and lined loaf tin and smooth out the dough. Place in the preheated oven and bake for 50–60 minutes.

6 Use the skewer test (see page 113) to ensure the loaf is cooked through. Allow to cool in the tin slightly, then pass a sharp knife around the edge of the tin and turn out the loaf on to a serving platter. Herb and Olive Bread does not keep well for very long as it tends to dry out, so consume it within two days.

POTATO FLOUR BREAD

3 eggs, medium-sized, separated

250 ml buttermilk (or plain yogurt)

1 tablespoon vegetable oil, plus
extra for greasing

250 g potato flour

100 g maize meal (or cornmeal)

3 teaspoons gluten-free baking powder

1 teaspoon sugar

½ teaspoon salt

Serves 6–8

This versatile bread is made quickly and easily and is suitable for toasting or for making sandwiches.

1 Preheat the oven to 190°C, gas mark 5. Grease an 11 x 21 cm non-stick loaf tin with a little oil and line it with baking parchment.

2 Whisk the egg yolks, buttermilk (or yogurt) and oil in a large bowl. Sift in the potato flour, maize meal, baking powder, sugar and salt and mix well.

3 In a separate bowl, beat the egg whites until stiff but not too dry. Mix a third of this into the batter to loosen it a little, then fold in the rest.

4 Pour the mixture into the prepared loaf tin. Place in the preheated oven and bake for 45 minutes. Use the skewer test (see page 113) to ensure the bread is cooked. Remove from the oven and allow to cool in the tin, then run a knife around the edge of the tin to loosen the loaf. Turn out and slice.

CORNBREAD

Made from maize meal and soured milk, this simple, rustic savoury bread (see above) is delicious served alone as a snack, or with stews.

1 Preheat the oven to 200°C, gas mark 6. Grease a square 20 cm cake tin with a little oil.

2 Melt the fat in a small saucepan over low heat, then leave to cool. Mix the maize meal, salt, baking powder and bicarbonate of soda in a bowl.

3 Add the soured milk or buttermilk, beaten eggs and melted fat. Mix together all of the ingredients until thoroughly combined.

4 Pour into the greased cake tin and bake in the preheated oven for 30 minutes. The bread should be firm to the touch when ready. Serve either warm or cold, cut into squares.

Oil for greasing

125 g bacon fat, dripping or margarine

175 g maize meal (or cornmeal or fine polenta)

1 teaspoon salt

1 teaspoon gluten-free baking powder

½ teaspoon bicarbonate of soda

200 ml milk with squeeze of lemon juice or buttermilk

2 eggs, medium-sized, beaten

Serves 6

The analysis for each recipe refers to a single serving, unless stated otherwise. Optional ingredients are not included. The figures are intended as a guide only. If salt is given in a measured amount in the recipe it has been included in the analysis; if the recipe suggests a pinch of salt or seasoning to taste, salt has not been included.

p.12 Tzatziki
80Kcals; 4.5g protein; 6.0g total fat; 13g saturated fat; 2.5g carbohydrate; 0.05g fibre; 47mg sodium; 109mg calcium

p.12 Hummus
284Kcals; 8g protein; 23g total fat; 3g saturated fat; 10g carbohydrate; 3.5g fibre; 16mg sodium; 154mg calcium

p.12 Guacamole
152Kcals; 2g protein; 14g total fat; 3g saturated fat; 4g carbohydrate; 3g fibre; 8mg sodium; 16mg calcium

p.13 Tapenade
224Kcals; 4g protein; 23g total fat; 3g saturated fat; 0g carbohydrate; 2.5g fibre; 2460mg sodium; 91mg calcium

p.14 Melon & Yogurt Soup
72Kcals; 3g protein; 0.5g total fat; 0.2g saturated fat; 15g carbohydrate; 1.5g fibre; 80mg sodium; 91mg calcium

p.14 Gazpacho
281Kcals; 2.5g protein; 24g total fat; 3.5g saturated fat; 11g carbohydrate; 3.5g fibre; 27mg sodium; 31mg calcium

p.14 Ajo Blanco
510Kcals; 10.5g protein; 50g total fat; 5.5g saturated fat; 4g carbohydrate; 4g fibre; 7mg sodium; 120mg calcium

p.16 Carrot & Orange Soup
82Kcals; 1.5g protein; 4g total fat; 0.5g saturated fat; 10g carbohydrate; 2g fibre; 157mg sodium; 38mg calcium

p.16 Aubergine Soup
180Kcals; 4g protein; 12.5g total fat; 2g saturated fat; 14g carbohydrate; 7g fibre; 192mg sodium; 47mg calcium

p.17 Spinach & Lemon Soup
136Kcals; 4.5g protein; 11g total fat; 7g saturated fat; 4g carbohydrate; 3g fibre; 450mg sodium; 224mg calcium

p.17 Rich Tomato Soup
94Kcals; 2.5g protein; 4g total fat; 0.1g saturated fat; 13g carbohydrate; 4g fibre; 52mg sodium; 49mg calcium

p.18 Sweetcorn Soup with Chilli
429Kcals; 4.5g protein; 33.5g total fat; 10g saturated fat; 29g carbohydrate; 2g fibre; 725mg sodium; 18mg calcium

p.19 Avgolemono Soup
114Kcals; 5g protein; 6g total fat; 1.5g saturated fat; 10.5g carbohydrate; 0g fibre; 370mg sodium; 32mg calcium

p.19 Fish Soup with Artichokes
55–44Kcals; 10–8g protein; 0.4–0.3g total fat; 0g saturated fat; 3–2g carbohydrate; 0g fibre; 370–296 mg sodium; 10–8mg calcium

p.20 Squid Salad
596Kcals; 19g protein; 57g total fat; 8g saturated fat; 1g carbohydrate; 0g fibre; 138mg sodium; 16mg calcium

p.20 Seafood Salad
217Kcals; 34g protein; 8.5g total fat; 1.5g saturated fat; 1g carbohydrate; 0.5g fibre; 355mg sodium; 218mg calcium

p.21 Prawn & Melon Salad
340Kcals; 23g protein; 24g total fat; 3.5g saturated fat; 7g carbohydrate; 1g fibre; 414mg sodium; 123mg calcium

p.23 Mussels with Salsa
60Kcals; 55g protein; 3.5g total fat; 0.5g saturated fat; 2g carbohydrate; 0.7g fibre; 66mg sodium; 65mg calcium

p.23 Sweetcorn Fritters
290Kcals; 7g protein; 18g total fat; 4g saturated fat; 26g carbohydrate; 1g fibre; 248mg sodium; 25mg calcium

p.24 Spinach Roulade
319Kcals; 13g protein; 28g total fat; 16g saturated fat; 3g carbohydrate; 2.5g fibre; 551mg sodium; 282mg calcium

p.25 Moulded Gazpacho
50Kcals; 0.5g protein; 4g total fat; 0.5g saturated fat; 3g carbohydrate; 1g fibre; 6mg sodium; 8mg calcium

p.26 Egg & Cucumber Terrine
150Kcals; 9g protein; 11g total fat; 3g saturated fat; 4g carbohydrate;

0.5g fibre; 119mg sodium; 125mg calcium

p.26 Chicken Liver Pâté
165–111Kcals; 11–7.5g protein; 12–8g total fat; 7–5g saturated fat; 2–1g carbohydrate; 0.3–0.2g fibre; 142–95mg sodium; 13–9mg calcium

p.28 Avocado Mousse & Prawn Sauce
390Kcals; 20g protein; 33g total fat; 6g saturated fat; 3g carbohydrate; 2g fibre; 1201mg sodium; 157mg calcium

p.29 Fish Mousse
140Kcals; 18g protein; 6g total fat; 2g saturated fat; 3g carbohydrate; 0g fibre; 886mg sodium; 92mg calcium

p.32 Baked Cod with Tomatoes
290Kcals; 42g protein; 10.5g total fat; 2g saturated fat; 7g carbohydrate; 2g fibre; 175mg sodium; 54mg calcium

p.33 Fish Pie
563Kcals; 44g protein; 21g total fat; 11g saturated fat; 52g carbohydrate; 2.5g fibre; 823mg sodium; 398mg calcium

p.34 Chicken with Basil & Almonds
543Kcals; 39g protein; 41g total fat; 13g saturated fat; 5g carbohydrate; 2g fibre; 157mg sodium; 176mg calcium

p.34 Chicken, Avocado & Yogurt Mayonnaise
628Kcals; 57g protein; 45g total fat; 10g saturated fat; 6g carbohydrate; 2.5g fibre; 309mg sodium; 127mg calcium

p.35 Chicken Fried with Rosemary & Garlic
382Kcals; 31g protein; 28g total fat; 7g saturated fat; 0g carbohydrate; 0g fibre; 138mg sodium; 13mg calcium

p.36 Chicory & Ham Gratin
395Kcals; 25g protein; 31g total fat; 19g saturated fat; 4g carbohydrate; 1g fibre; 797mg sodium; 554mg calcium

p.36 Beef Pie with Olives & Raisins
675–450Kcals; 36–24g protein; 33–22g total fat; 9–6g saturated fat; 61–41g carbohydrate; 5–3g fibre; 784–522mg sodium; 116–77mg calcium

p.37 Beef Salad with Mustard Dressing
590Kcals; 42g protein; 46g total fat; 12g saturated fat; 1g carbohydrate; 0g fibre; 86mg sodium; 24mg calcium

p.37 Pork with Tuna & Yogurt Sauce
272Kcals; 52g protein; 11g total fat; 3g saturated fat; 2g carbohydrate; 232g fibre; 0mg sodium; 59mg calcium

p.39 Soufflé
320Kcals; 18g protein; 24g total fat; 13g saturated fat; 7.5g carbohydrate; 0g fibre; 375mg sodium; 33mg calcium

p.40 Cheese & Onion Tart
868–580Kcals; 27–18g protein; 45–30g total fat; 24–16g saturated fat; 85–66g carbohydrate; 3–2g fibre; 404–270mg sodium; 247–165mg calcium

p.41 Tortilla
295Kcals; 11g protein; 19g total fat; 4g saturated fat; 21g carbohydrate; 2g fibre; 107mg sodium; 52mg calcium

p.43 Risotto
456Kcals; 12g protein; 15g total fat; 9g saturated fat; 62g carbohydrate; 0.5g fibre; 618mg sodium; 182mg calcium

p.44 Risotto Croquettes
224Kcals; 6g protein; 12g total fat; 4g saturated fat; 21g carbohydrate; 0.5g fibre; 227mg sodium; 69mg calcium

p.44 Asparagus Risotto
382Kcals; 8g protein; 8.5g total fat; 1.5g saturated fat; 67g carbohydrate; 1g fibre; 366mg sodium; 62mg calcium

p.46 Polenta
115Kcals; 3g protein; 1g total fat; 0g saturated fat; 23g carbohydrate; 0.7g fibre; 246mg sodium; 1mg calcium

p.47 Polenta Gnocchi
462Kcals; 23g protein; 23g total fat; 12g saturated fat; 41g carbohydrate; 1g fibre; 415mg sodium; 607mg calcium

p.48 Lentil & Grilled Pepper Salad
(For the salad only) 50–200Kcals; 17–13.5g protein; 4.5–3.5g total fat; 1–0.5g saturated fat; 39–31g carbohydrate; 9–7g fibre; 15–12 mg sodium; 69–55mg calcium

(For the dressing: 1 tbsp) 99Kcals; 0g protein; 11g fat; 1.5g saturated fat; 0g carbohydrate, 0g fibre, 0g sodium; 0g calcium

p.49 Lentil & Bacon Stew
532–425Kcals; 26–21g protein; 32–26g total fat; 11–8.5g saturated fat; 37–29g carbohydrate; 7–5.5g fibre; 989–791mg sodium; 72–58mg calcium

p.49 Chickpea Salad with Tuna & Onions
200–160Kcals; 19.5–15.5g protein; 5–4g total fat; 1–0.7g saturated fat; 19–15g carbohydrate; 4–4.5g fibre; 245–196mg sodium; 60–48mg calcium

p.52 Seafood Paella
550Kcals; 28g protein; 10g total fat; 1.5g saturated fat; 59g carbohydrate; 1g fibre; 247mg sodium; 182mg calcium

p.54 Fish Pilaf
520Kcals; 35g protein; 14g total fat; 3g saturated fat; 62g carbohydrate; 0g fibre; 1015mg sodium; 74mg calcium

p.55 Swordfish in Caper & Tomato Sauce
240Kcals; 42g protein; 9g total fat; 2g saturated fat; 7g carbohydrate; 2g fibre; 234mg sodium; 24mg calcium

p.56 Poached Chicken & Vegetables with Red & Green Sauces
(Chicken & vegetables only)
554Kcals; 62g protein; 15g total fat; 5g saturated fat; 44g carbohydrate; 7g fibre; 189mg sodium; 92mg calcium
Salsa Verde 235Kcals; 29g protein; 22g total fat; 2.5g saturated fat; 4g carbohydrate; 4g fibre; 517mg sodium; 194mg calcium
Salsa Rossa 114Kcals; 1.5g protein; 9g total fat; 1g saturated fat; 8g carbohydrate; 2g fibre; 10mg sodium; 18mg calcium

p.58 Chicken Breasts Rolled with Ham & Cheese
400Kcals; 40g protein; 22g total fat; 9g saturated fat; 3g carbohydrate; 0.5g fibre; 417mg sodium; 202mg calcium

p.59 Chicken Breasts Stuffed with Ricotta
410Kcals; 43g protein; 22g total fat; 10g saturated fat; 3g carbohydrate; 0.3g fibre; 303mg sodium; 256mg calcium

p.60 Spiced Beef Casserole
350–261Kcals; 39–29g protein; 12–9g total fat; 4–3g saturated fat; 19–14g carbohydrate; 2.4–2g fibre; 122–91mg sodium; 31–23mg calcium

p.60 Braised Steak with Mushrooms
350Kcals; 37g protein; 15g total fat; 5g saturated fat; 3g carbohydrate; 1g fibre; 10mg sodium; 29mg calcium

p.61 Marinated Beef with Olives
470Kcals; 39g protein; 32g total fat; 7g saturated fat; 2g carbohydrate; 1g fibre; 659mg sodium; 26mg calcium

p.62 Stuffed Peppers
340Kcals; 19g protein; 18g total fat; 4g saturated fat; 26g carbohydrate; 3g fibre; 123mg sodium; 116mg calcium

p.63 Meatballs in Tomato & Mushroom Sauce
435–350Kcals; 34–27g protein; 26–21g total fat; 8.5–7g saturated fat; 7–5.5g carbohydrate; 0.7–0.5g fibre; 552–418mg sodium; 40–32mg calcium

p.64 Moroccan Lamb
480Kcals; 44g protein; 21g total fat; 9g saturated fat; 1g carbohydrate; 0g fibre; 486mg sodium; 41mg calcium

p.64 Moussaka
775Kcals; 59g protein; 51g total fat; 20g saturated fat; 22g carbohydrate; 5g fibre; 308mg sodium; 207mg calcium

p.66 Marinated & Grilled Lamb
370Kcals; 35g protein; 25g total fat; 8g saturated fat; 0g carbohydrate; 0g fibre; 123mg sodium; 21mg calcium

p.67 Braised Lamb with Aubergine
390–315Kcals; 38–31g protein; 23–19g total fat; 8–6g saturated fat; 7–5.5g carbohydrate; 3–2g fibre; 494–396mg sodium; 52–41mg calcium

p.68 Pork Fillet with Apricots
511Kcals; 41g protein; 16g total fat; 5g saturated fat; 31g carbohydrate; 4g fibre; 453mg sodium; 66mg calcium

p.68 Pork Loin Stuffed with Pâté
527Kcals; 58g protein; 31g total fat; 11.5g saturated fat; 2.4g

carbohydrate; 0g fibre; 1181mg sodium; 28mg calcium

p.72 Potato Gratin
290Kcals; 6g protein; 17g total fat; 11g saturated fat; 30g carbohydrate; 2g fibre; 181mg sodium; 106mg calcium

p.72 Mashed Potatoes with Olive Oil
211Kcals; 4.5g protein; 9g total fat; 2g saturated fat; 30g carbohydrate; 2g fibre; 30mg sodium; 47mg calcium

p.73 Potato Soufflé
400Kcals; 12g protein; 26g total fat; 14g saturated fat; 29g carbohydrate; 2g fibre; 245mg sodium; 65mg calcium

p.73 Spicy Potatoes in Tomato Sauce
215–144Kcals; 4–3g protein; 9–6g total fat; 1–1g saturated fat; 30–20g carbohydrate; 3–2g fibre; 47–32mg sodium; 23–15mg calcium

p.74 Rösti
160Kcals; 3g protein; 5g total fat; 2g saturated fat; 26g carbohydrate; 2g fibre; 29mg sodium; 8mg calcium

p.74 Roast Potatoes with Rosemary & Garlic
211–141Kcals; 3–2g protein; 11–7.5g total fat; 1.5–1g saturated fat; 26–17g carbohydrate; 2–1.3g fibre; 11–7mg sodium; 8–5mg calcium

p.76 Mushrooms with Lemon & Thyme
54Kcals; 1g protein; 5.5g total fat; 1g saturated fat; 0g carbohydrate; 0g fibre; 48mg sodium; 18mg calcium

p.77 Mushrooms Stuffed with Parmesan Cheese
95Kcals; 4g protein; 9g total fat; 2g saturated fat; 3g carbohydrate; 1g fibre; 72mg sodium; 80mg calcium

p.77 Black-eye Beans with Mushrooms
220–150Kcals; 16–11g protein; 2.5–1.5g total fat; 0.5–0.3g saturated fat; 36–24g carbohydrate; 6–4g fibre; 14–9mg sodium; 61–40mg calcium

p.78 Roasted Vegetables
170–115Kcals; 3.5–2g protein; 12–8g total fat; 2–1g saturated fat; 13–9g carbohydrate; 3.5–5g fibre;

15–10mg sodium; 47–31mg calcium

p.79 Roasted Pepper Salad
90–60Kcals; 2–1g protein; 3.5–2.5g total fat; 0.5–0.5g saturated fat; 13–8.5g carbohydrate; 3–2g fibre; 8–5mg sodium; 16–11mg calcium

p.79 Fried Peppers
125–83Kcals; 1.4–1g protein; 11.5–8g total fat; 2–1g saturated fat; 4.5–3g carbohydrate; 2.8–2g fibre; 7–5mg sodium; 14–9mg calcium

p.80 Fennel with Cheese Sauce
205Kcals; 10g protein; 14g total fat; 9g saturated fat; 11g carbohydrate; 2g fibre; 240mg sodium; 289mg calcium

p.81 Courgette & Sesame Gratin
172Kcals; 9g protein; 14g total fat; 6g saturated fat; 2g carbohydrate; 1.5g fibre; 170mg sodium; 237mg calcium

p.81 Aubergine Gratin
421Kcals; 22g protein; 33g total fat; 17.5g saturated fat; 8g carbohydrate; 6.5g fibre; 513mg sodium; 574mg calcium

p.82 Green Beans with Garlic & Almonds
155Kcals; 5g protein; 13g total fat; 1.5g saturated fat; 5g carbohydrate; 4g fibre; 2mg sodium; 75mg calcium

p.82 Fennel with Beans
250Kcals; 15g protein; 6.5g total fat; 1g saturated fat; 34g carbohydrate; 6g fibre; 15mg sodium; 61mg calcium

p.83 Broad Beans & Ham
226Kcals; 19g protein; 8g total fat; 1g saturated fat; 19g carbohydrate; 15g fibre; 253mg sodium; 61mg calcium

p.84 Chickpeas with Spinach
245–163Kcals; 11–7g protein; 15–10g total fat; 2–1.5g saturated fat; 18–12g carbohydrate; 7–4.5g fibre; 395–263mg sodium; 257–170mg calcium

p.85 Vegetable 'Spaghetti'
76–60Kcals; 1.5–1g protein; 6–4g total fat; 1–0.5g saturated fat; 4–3g carbohydrate; 2–1g fibre; 8–6mg sodium; 27–18mg calcium

p.85 Carrots with Cumin
72–58Kcals; 1.5–1g protein; 3–2.5g total fat; 0.5–0.4g saturated fat; 10–8g carbohydrate; 3–2.5g fibre;

212–169mg sodium; 34–28mg calcium

p.86 Tomato & Artichoke Salad
60–40Kcals; 7.5–5g protein; 0.7–0.5g total fat; 0.3–0.2g saturated fat; 9–6g carbohydrate; 0.8–0.5g fibre; 74–50mg sodium; 108–72mg calcium

p.86 Tomatoes Stuffed with Herb Rice
100Kcals; 3g protein; 5g total fat; 1g saturated fat; 11g carbohydrate; 1g fibre; 30mg sodium; 22mg calcium

p.87 Tomatoes Baked with Parmesan Cheese
120Kcals; 5g protein; 10g total fat; 3.5g saturated fat; 1.5g carbohydrate; 0.5g fibre; 140mg sodium; 154mg calcium

p.88 Lettuce Hearts with Anchovy Dressing
258Kcals; 2.5g protein; 27g total fat; 3.5g saturated fat; 0.5g carbohydrate; 0g fibre; 371mg sodium; 32mg calcium

p.88 Carrots with Raisins & Pine Kernels
291–194Kcals; 3–2g protein; 23–15g total fat; 3–2g saturated fat; 19–13g carbohydrate; 3.5–2g fibre; 90–60mg sodium; 39–26mg calcium

p.90 Mayonnaise
(per 15 ml) 100Kcals; 0.2g protein; 11g total fat; 1.5g saturated fat; 0g carbohydrate; 0g fibre; 76mg sodium; 2mg calcium

p.90 Pesto
(per 15 ml) 120Kcals; 2g protein; 12g total fat; 2g saturated fat; 1g carbohydrate; 0g fibre; 42mg sodium; 73mg calcium

p.91 White Sauce
287Kcals; 10g protein; 12g total fat; 7g saturated fat; 37g carbohydrate; 0g fibre; 178mg sodium; 349mg calcium

p.91 Vinaigrette
(per 15 ml) 83Kcals; 0g protein; 9g total fat; 1g saturated fat; 0g carbohydrate; 0g fibre; 22mg sodium; 0mg calcium

p.94 Rice Pudding Brûlée
243Kcals; 6g protein; 5g total fat; 3g saturated fat; 42g carbohydrate; 0g fibre; 69mg sodium; 149mg calcium

p.94 Fruit Salad Brûlée
190Kcals; 1g protein; 12g total fat; 7.5g saturated fat; 21g carbohydrate; 1g fibre; 12mg sodium; 25mg calcium

p.95 Apricot Soufflé
200–135Kcals; 10–6.5g protein; 8–5g total fat; 2.5–2g saturated fat; 24.5–16g carbohydrate; 3.5–2.5g fibre; 103–69mg sodium; 76–51mg calcium

p.95 Hot Fruit Salad
170Kcals; 1.5g protein; 8g total fat; 5g saturated fat; 25g carbohydrate; 2g fibre; 75mg sodium; 34mg calcium

p.97 Pears Baked in Custard
600–400Kcals; 10–7g protein; 46–31g total fat; 25–17g saturated fat; 39–26g carbohydrate; 5–3.5g fibre; 130–87mg sodium; 107–71mg calcium

p.97 Figs in Honey & Wine
166Kcals; 1.5g protein; 0g total fat; 0g saturated fat; 34g carbohydrate; 1.5g fibre; 8mg sodium; 44mg calcium

p.98 Honey-Poached Oranges
120Kcals; 1.5g protein; 0g total fat; 0g saturated fat; 31g carbohydrate; 2g fibre; 8mg sodium; 57mg calcium

p.98 Orange & Date Salad
130–85Kcals; 3–2g protein; 0g total fat; 0g saturated fat; 30–20g carbohydrate; 5–3g fibre; 15–10mg sodium; 129–86mg calcium

p.98 Orange Crème Caramel
(Using all milk) 230Kcals; 8g protein; 8g total fat; 3g saturated fat; 35g carbohydrate; 0g fibre; 104mg sodium; 120mg calcium

p.101 Vanilla Cheesecake
420–315Kcals; 17–13g protein; 19–14g total fat; 11–8g saturated fat; 47–35g carbohydrate; 0g fibre; 626–469mg sodium; 106–80mg calcium

p.102 Apple Tart
418Kcals; 4g protein; 15g total fat; 9g saturated fat; 68g carbohydrate; 2.5g fibre; 147mg sodium; 18mg calcium

p.103 Lemon Custard Tart
470Kcals; 10g protein; 29g total fat; 16g saturated fat; 44g carbohydrate; 0.6g fibre; 146mg sodium; 48mg calcium

p.104 Almond Meringue Gâteau
500Kcals; 8g protein; 34g total fat; 13g saturated fat; 43g carbohydrate; 2g fibre; 60mg sodium; 83mg calcium

p.105 Rolled Coconut Meringue
475–356Kcals; 4–3g protein; 25–19g total fat; 18.5–14g saturated fat; 61–46g carbohydrate; 2.5–2g fibre; 94–71mg sodium; 24–18mg calcium

p.106 Vanilla Ice Cream
225Kcals; 4.5g protein; 19g total fat; 11g saturated fat; 9g carbohydrate; 0g fibre; 58mg sodium; 39mg calcium

p.106 Chocolate Chip Ice Cream with Raspberry Sauce
375Kcals; 3.5g protein; 25g total fat; 15g saturated fat; 35g carbohydrate; 1g fibre; 49mg sodium; 39mg calcium

p.107 Strawberry Sorbet
90–59Kcals; 2.5–1.5g protein; 0g total fat; 0g saturated fat; 21–14g carbohydrate; 1.5–1g fibre; 38–25mg sodium; 21–14mg calcium

p.107 Coffee Praline Mousse
240Kcals; 10g protein; 14.5g total fat; 8g saturated fat; 18g carbohydrate; 0g fibre; 105mg sodium; 136mg calcium

p.108 Lemon Curd
(per 15 ml) 60Kcals; 1g protein; 3g total fat; 1.5g saturated fat; 8g carbohydrate; 0g fibre; 27mg sodium; 4mg calcium

p.108 Vanilla Custard
(per 600 ml) 663Kcals; 32g protein; 34g total fat; 16.5g saturated fat; 61g carbohydrate; 0g fibre; 468mg sodium; 681mg calcium

p.112 Chocolate Hazelnut Cake
1048–786–Kcals; 18–13.5g protein; 81–61g total fat; 34–25g saturated fat; 67–50g carbohydrate; 3–2g fibre; 374–281mg sodium; 176–132mg calcium

p.113 Chocolate Roulade
320Kcals; 5g protein; 21g total fat; 12g saturated fat; 28g carbohydrate; 0g fibre; 60mg sodium; 37mg calcium

p.114 Chocolate Walnut Cake
660–500Kcals; 20–15g protein; 44–33g total fat; 10–7g saturated fat; 50–37g carbohydrate; 1.5–1g fibre; 476–375mg sodium; 123–93mg calcium

p.114 Lemon Polenta & Almond Cake
772–580Kcals; 15–11g protein; 54–40g total fat; 22–17g saturated fat; 59–44g carbohydrate; 3–2.5g fibre; 435–326mg sodium; 120–90mg calcium

p.115 Almond Sponge Cake
410–305Kcals; 12.5–9g protein; 22.5–17g total fat; 3.5–2.5g saturated fat; 41–31g carbohydrate; 2–1.5g fibre; 82–61mg sodium; 100–75mg calcium

p.117 Orange & Almond Cake
515–390Kcals; 16–12g protein; 28–21g total fat; 4–3g saturated fat; 52–40g carbohydrate; 4–3g fibre; 100–75mg sodium; 159–119mg calcium

p.118 Date & Brown Sugar Muffins
(per large muffin) 270Kcals; 6.5g protein; 10g total fat; 5g saturated fat; 39g carbohydrate; 1g fibre; 212mg sodium; 73mg calcium

p.120 Fruit & Nut Loaf
610–460Kcals; 8–6g protein; 33–27g total fat; 20–15g saturated fat; 66–49g carbohydrate; 1.5–1g fibre; 393–295mg sodium; 36–27mg calcium

p.121 Sand Cake
580–435Kcals; 6–4.5g protein; 36–27g total fat; 20–15g saturated fat; 62–46g carbohydrate; 1–0.5g fibre; 317–238mg sodium; 48–36mg calcium

p.121 Rice Cake
275–210Kcals; 8–6g protein; 14–11g total fat; 8–6g saturated fat; 30–23g carbohydrate; 0g fibre; 157–118mg sodium; 118–89mg calcium

p.122 Herb & Olive Bread
350–260Kcals; 11–8g protein; 15.5–11.5g total fat; 3–2g saturated fat; 40–30g carbohydrate; 1.5–1g fibre; 862–647mg sodium; 96–72mg calcium

p.122 Potato Flour Bread
290–220Kcals; 11–8g protein; 7–5.5g total fat; 1.5–1g saturated fat; 47–35g carbohydrate; 3–2g fibre; 479–359mg sodium; 100–75mg calcium

p.123 Cornbread
340Cal; 6.5g protein; 24g total fat; 12g saturated fat; 23g carbohydrate; 0.5g fibre; 568mg sodium; 60mg calcium

Index

Entries in italics denote
variations on the main recipes

Ajo Blanco 14
Almond Meringue Gâteau 104
Almond Sponge Cake 115
Apples Baked in Custard 97
Apple Tart 102
Apricot(s)
    Dried Apricot Purée 109
    Muffins 118
    Pork Fillet with Apricots 68
    Soufflé 95
Artichoke(s)
    Fish Soup with Artichokes 19
    Tomato & Artichoke Salad 86
Asparagus Risotto 44
Aubergine(s)
    Braised Lamb with Aubergine
        67
        Gratin 81
    *Roasted with Sweet Potato and
        Spinach 78*
    Soup 16
    Stuffed 62
Avgolemono Soup 19
Avocado(s)
    Chicken, Avocado & Yogurt
        Mayonnaise 34
    Guacamole 12
    Guacamole Mousse 28
    Mousse & Prawn Sauce 28

Bacon and Cheese Tart 40
Baked Cod with Tomatoes 32
    Baked Fish Parcels 32
    Baked Halibut 32
    Baked Turbot 32
Banana Muffins 118
Beans
    Broad Bean Salad 83
    Broad Beans & Ham 83
    Fennel with Beans 82
    Green Beans with Garlic &
        Almonds 82
    with Hazelnuts 82
Beef (*see also* meat)
    Braised Steak with
        Mushrooms 60
    Marinated Beef with Olives
        61
    Pie with Olives & Raisins 36
    Salad with Mustard Dressing
        37
    Spiced Beef Casserole 60
Black-eye Beans with
    Mushrooms 77
Braised Lamb Chops 67
Braised Lamb with Aubergine
    67

Braised Steak with Mushrooms
    60
Breads
    Cornbread 123
    Herb & Olive Bread 122
    Potato Flour Bread 122
Broad Bean Salad 83
Broad Beans & Ham 83

Cakes
    Almond Sponge Cake 115
    Chocolate Hazelnut Cake 112
    Chocolate Walnut Cake 114
    Fruit & Nut Loaf 120
    Lemon Polenta & Almond
        Cake 114
    Orange & Almond Cake 117
    Rice Cake 121
    Sand Cake 121
    The Skewer Test 113
Carrot(s)
    with Apple and Dates 88
    with Cumin 85
    with Mango Chutney 85
    & Orange Soup 16
    with Raisins & Pine Kernels
        88
    Roasted Carrots and Parsnips 78
Cheese & Onion Tart 40
Chicken
    Avocado & Yogurt
        Mayonnaise 34
    with Basil & Almonds 34
    *Breasts Rolled with Goat's
        Cheese and Herbs 58*
    Breasts Rolled with Ham &
        Cheese 58
    Breasts Stuffed with Ricotta
        59
    Fried with Rosemary & Garlic
        35
    Liver Pâté 26
    Poached Chicken &
        Vegetables with Red &
        Green Sauces 56
Chickpea Salad with Tuna &
    Onions 49
Chickpeas with Spinach 84
Chicory & Ham Gratin 36
Chocolate
    Chip Ice Cream with
        Raspberry Sauce 106
    Hazelnut Cake 112
    Roulade 113
    Sauce 109
    Walnut Cake 114
Coffee Praline Mousse 107
Cornbread 123
Courgette & Sesame Gratin 81
Custard 108

Date & Brown Sugar Muffins
    118
Dips 12–13
Dressings
    Balsamic 48
    Mustard 37
    Vinaigrette 91

Egg & Cucumber Terrine 26

Fennel
    with Beans 82
    with Cheese Sauce 80
    Roasted 78
Figs in Honey & Wine 97
Fish
    Baked Cod with Tomatoes 32
    Baked Fish Parcels 32
    Baked Halibut 32
    Baked Turbot 32
    Chickpea Salad with Tuna &
        Onions 49
    *Cold Swordfish in Tomato
        Cream 55*
    Mousse 29
    Mussels with Salsa 23
    Pie 33
    Pilaf 54
    Prawn & Melon Salad 21
    Prawn Sauce 28
    Seafood Paella 52
    Seafood Salad 20
    Soup with Artichokes 19
    Squid Salad 20
    Stock 19, 52
    Swordfish in Caper & Tomato
        Sauce 55
Fried Peppers 79
Fruit (*see also* individual fruits)
    Coulis 109
    Hot Fruit Salad 95
    & Nut Loaf 120
    Salad Brûlée 94

Gazpacho 14
    Moulded 25
Glazes
    Pineapple 101
    Raspberry 101
Gratin
    Aubergine Gratin 81
    *Cauliflower with Cheese Sauce
        80*
    Chicory & Ham Gratin 36
    Courgette & Sesame Gratin
        81
    Fennel with Cheese Sauce 80
    Leeks with Cheese Sauce 80

Polenta au Gratin 51
    Potato Gratin 72
Green Beans with Garlic &
    Almonds 82
    with Hazelnuts 82
Guacamole 12
    Guacamole Mousse 28

Ham Mousse 29
Herb & Olive Bread 122
Honey-poached Oranges 98
Hot Fruit Salad 95
Hummus 12

Ice Cream
    Chocolate Chip Ice Cream
        with Raspberry Sauce 106
    Vanilla Ice Cream 106

Lamb (*see also* Meat)
    Braised Lamb Chops 67
    Braised Lamb with Aubergine
        67
    Kebabs 66
    Marinated & Grilled Lamb 66
    Moroccan Lamb 64
    Moussaka 64
Lemon
    Curd 108
    Custard Tart 103
    Polenta & Almond Cake 114
    Sauce 91
    Spinach & Lemon Soup 17
Lentil(s)
    & Bacon Stew 49
    & Grilled Pepper Salad 48
Lettuce Hearts with Anchovy
    Dressing 88

Marinated Beef with Olives 61
Marinated & Grilled Lamb 66
Mashed Potatoes with Olive Oil
    72
Mayonnaise 90
    Garlic 90
    Green (Watercress) 90
    Saffron 19
    Tuna Fish (Tonnato) 90
    Yogurt 34
Meat (*see also* Beef, Lamb, Pork)
    Meatballs in Tomato &
        Mushroom Sauce 63
    Meat Loaf 63
    Stuffed Peppers 62
Melon
    Prawn & Melon Salad 21
    & Yogurt Soup 14

Meringue(s)
Almond Meringue Gâteau 104
Nests 105
Preparation 105
Rolled Coconut Meringue 105
Moroccan Lamb 64
Moulded Gazpacho 25
Moussaka 64
Mousse
Avocado Mousse with Prawn Sauce 28
Coffee Praline Mousse 107
Fish Mousse 29
Guacamole Mousse 28
Ham Mousse 29
Muffins
Apricot 118
Banana 118
Date & Brown Sugar Muffins 118
Raisin 118
Savoury Cheese 118
Mushroom(s)
Black-eye Beans with Mushrooms 77
Braised Steak with Mushrooms 60
with Lemon & Thyme 76
Meatballs in Mushroom & Tomato Sauce 63
Risotto 44
with Serano Ham and Chilli 76
Stuffed with Parmesan Cheese 77
Vegetable-stuffed 77
Mussels with Salsa 23

Orange(s)
& Almond Cake 117
Carrot & Orange Soup 16
Crème Caramel 98
& Date Salad 98
Honey-poached Oranges 98

Pâté
Chicken Liver Pâté 26
Pork Loin Stuffed with Pâté 68
Pears Baked in Custard 97
Pepper(s)
Fried Peppers 79
Lentil & Grilled Pepper Salad 48
Pepper, Tomato and Anchovy Relish 79
Roasted Pepper Salad 79
Stuffed Peppers 62
Pesto 90
Rice 59
Tomato 90
Pineapple Glaze 101
Poached Chicken & Vegetables with Red & Green Sauces 56
Polenta
Croutons 47
Gnocchi 47
au Gratin 47

Lemon Polenta & Almond Cake 114
Pork (*see also* Meat)
Fillet with Apricots 68
Ham Mousse 29
Loin Stuffed with Pâté 68
with Tuna & Yogurt Sauce 37
Potato(es)
Flour Bread 122
Gratin 72
Mashed with Olive Oil 72
Roast Potatoes with Rosemary & Garlic 74
Roasted Sweet Potatoes and Aubergine with Spinach 78
Rösti 74
Soufflé 73
Spicy Potatoes in Tomato Sauce 73
Spicy Sweet Potatoes 73
Prawn & Melon Salad 21
Praline 107
Pulses
Chickpea Salad with Tuna & Onions 49
Lentil & Bacon Stew 49
Lentil & Grilled Pepper Salad 48
Preparation 85

Raisin Muffins 118
Raspberry
Glaze 101
Sauce 106
Rice (*see also* Risotto)
Cake 121
Fish Pilaf 54
Flavouring Long-grain Rice 43
Pesto Rice 59
Preparation 43
Pudding Brûlée 94
Seafood Paella 52
Spicy Moroccan Rice 68
Tomatoes Stuffed with Herb Rice 86
Rich Tomato Soup 17
Risotto 43
Asparagus 44
Croquettes 44
Mushroom 44
Roast Potatoes with Rosemary & Garlic 74
Roasted Pepper Salad 79
Roasted Vegetables 78
Aubergine & Sweet Potato with Spinach 78
Carrots & Parsnips 78
Fennel 78
Rolled Coconut Meringue 105
Rösti 74

Saffron
Dried and Powdered 19
Mayonnaise 19
Salads
Chickpea Salad with Tuna & Onions 49

Lentil & Grilled Pepper Salad 49
Lettuce Hearts with Anchovy Dressing 88
Prawn & Melon Salad 21
Seafood Salad 20
Squid Salad 20
Tomato & Artichoke Salad 86
Sand Cake 121
Sauces
Caper 91
Cheese 91
Chilli (with sweetcorn soup) 18
Chocolate 109
Lemon 91
Marmalade 117
Onion 91
Parsley 91
Prawn 28 (with avocado mousse)
Raspberry 106
Rossa (red) 56
Tomato 55
Tomato & Mushroom (with meatballs) 63
Verde (Green) 56
White 33, 91
Yogurt & Tuna (with pork) 37
Savoury Cheese Muffins 118
Seafood (*see* Fish)
Soufflé 39
Apricot Soufflé 95
Flavourings 39
Potato Soufflé 73
Soups
Ajo Blanco 14
Aubergine 16
Avgolemono 19
Carrot & Orange 16
Fish Soup with Artichokes 19
Gazpacho 14
Melon & Yogurt 14
Rich Tomato 17
Spinach & Lemon 17
Sweetcorn Soup with Chilli Sauce 18
Spiced Beef Casserole 60
Spicy Potatoes in Tomato Sauce 73
Spicy Sweet Potatoes 73
Spinach & Lemon Soup 17
Spinach Roulade 24
Squid Salad 20
Strawberry Sorbet 107
Stuffed Aubergine 62
Stuffed Peppers 62
Stuffed Tomatoes 62
Sweetcorn Fritters 23
Sweetcorn Soup with Chilli Sauce 18
Swordfish in Caper & Tomato Sauce 55
Cold Swordfish in Tomato 55

Tapenade 13
Tarts
Apple Tart 102
Bacon and Cheese Tart 40

Cheese & Onion Tart 40
Lemon Custard Tart 103
Tomato(es)
& Artichoke Salad 86
Baked Cod with Tomatoes 32
Baked with Parmesan Cheese 87
Meatballs in Tomato & Mushroom Sauce 63
Pesto 90
Rich Tomato Soup 17
Sauce 55
Spicy Potatoes with Tomato Sauce 73
Stuffed with Herb Rice 86
Stuffed with Meat 62
Stuffed with Tuna 86
Tortilla 41
Tzatziki 12

Vanilla
Cheesecake 101
Custard 108
Ice Cream 106
Vegetable(s) (*see also* individual vegetables)
Chickpeas with Spinach 84
Chicory & Ham Gratin 36
Courgette & Sesame Gratin 81
Roasted 78
'Spaghetti' 85
Spinach Roulade 24
Sweetcorn Fritters 23
Vinaigrette 91

White Sauce 91

Yogurt
Mayonnaise 34
& Melon Soup 14
Pork with Tuna & Yogurt Sauce 37

ACKNOWLEDGEMENTS

Carroll & Brown would particularly like to thank The Coeliac Society for their expert advice.

Food preparation: Michael Cox
Art director: Denise Brown
Nutritional analysis: Fiona Hunter

Thanks also to Laura Price, Dawn Henderson and Charlotte Beech for their assistance.